HAPPINESS UNLIMITED

HAPPINESS UNLIMITED

Conversational Adaptation from the Internationally Acclaimed TV Series

AWAKENING WITH BRAHMA KUMARIS

Published by

THIRD EYE

Exclusively for

MANJUL

Manjul Publishing House

First published in India by

THIRD EYE

An imprint of **Pentagon Press**

206, Peacock Lane,

Shahpur Jat, New Delhi, INDIA-110 049

Exclusively for

Manjul Publishing House Pvt. Ltd.

•2nd Floor, Usha Preet Complex,

42 Malviya Nagar, Bhopal 462 003 - India

•7/32, Ground Floor, Ansari Road, Daryaganj, New Delhi 110 002

Email: manjul@manjulindia.com Website: www.manjulindia.com

Distribution Centres

Ahmedabad, Bengaluru, Bhopal, Kolkata, Chennai,

Hyderabad, Mumbai, New Delhi, Pune

HAPPINESS UNLIMITED

Awakening with Brahma Kumaris

This edition first published in 2015

Fifth impression 2015

ISBN 978-81-8274-826-2

Printed and bound in India by Thomson Press (India) Ltd.

Contents

Introduction	*vii*
Note to the Reader	*xi*

BOOK 1: 'CHOOSING HAPPINESS'

It is the Choice I Make	3
To Create the Thought, to Embrace the Journey	17
First, I Will Take Care of Myself	30
I Do Not Want Peace I Am Peace	42

BOOK 2: 'CHOOSING AWARENESS'

I Have to Be Happy First	57
Just One Thought Away	70
I Am Aware. I Am Creating	84
Think. Believe. The Rest Will Follow	96
Creating my Destiny	107
The Energy of Consciousness	119

Everything Happens Here (In the Mind)   131
The Colour of My Thoughts   142
To Heal You, I Have to Be Healed First   154

Brahma Kumaris   167

vi

Introduction

An international daily TV talk show, *Awakening with Brahma Kumaris* is changing people's lives all over the world. The programme is designed to have a simple and practical focus, so as to empower people to take charge of their lives and awaken them to their pure inner selves. The purpose of the programme is to give an insight into how and why we think and behave in certain ways. The process reveals many of our subconscious beliefs and perceptions that control our thoughts and feelings and the consequent behaviours, and then takes us on a journey of self-transformation.

The programme – a household name today – has helped people overcome mental stress, depression, addictions, low self-esteem and unhappy relationships, as they take personal responsibility for their lives, alter their outlook towards challenges, and become solution-oriented.

The source of knowledge of all that is discussed on the programme is the Brahma Kumaris, which is an international NGO in general consultative status with the Economic and Social Council of the United Nations and in consultative status with UNICEF. With its global headquarters in Mt. Abu, Rajasthan, through more than 8,500 centers in over 133 countries, the Brahma Kumaris offer a wide range of courses and programs to create positive change.

The Brahma Kumaris teaches Rajyoga as a way of experiencing peace of mind and a positive approach to life. The organisation provides opportunities to people from all religious and cultural backgrounds to explore their own spirituality and learn skills of reflection and meditation derived from Rajyoga, which will help develop inner calm, clear thinking and personal well-being.

At the heart of the organisation's teachings is the foundation course in HYPERLINK "http://www.bkwsu. org/whatwedo/courses/fcirym" Raja Yoga Meditation. This course provides a logical and practical understanding of the relationship between spirit and matter, as well as an understanding of the interplay between souls, God and the material world. All courses, seminar and workshops are offered to the public free of charge, as a community service. HYPERLINK "http://www.bkwsu.org/" www.bkwsu.org (International), HYPERLINK "http://www.brahmakumaris. com/" www.brahmakumaris.com (India)

This book is the first of a series that will attempt to bring readers close to the heart of this spiritual movement that has been going from strength to evermore strength since it was founded in 1936 by benign millionaire diamond merchant

Lekhraj Khubchand. The subject of each book will be brought home to you, the reader, through conversations that will touch, seek, shake, and probe deep into life's questions and dilemmas.

HAPPINESS UNLIMITED

The reason why there is so little happiness in the world is dependency. And this is the irony. Because happiness is not dependent on 'anything' or 'anyone' or found 'anywhere'.

Happiness is only possible when we are able to accept everyone as they are. That means an end to judging or resisting others, an end to complaining and blaming, an end to criticising and controlling, and an end to competing with anyone.

It is only when we choose thoughts and feelings aligned with our true state of purity, peace and love that we shift from: asking to sharing; holding on to letting go; expectations to acceptance; past and future to being in the now. We create a life of joy, contentment and bliss, because we have the choice and the power. **Happiness is a decision.**

That is the thought motif that will be pursued in the conversation that is to unfold between Suresh Oberoi, the internationally recognised Indian cinema actor, and Sister Shivani, a practitioner of Rajyoga Meditation of the Brahma Kumaris. By no means is it a linear conversation. Moments of clarity intersperse with mirages of certain bliss – but that distinction is precisely what the mind has to move toward grasping.

This is not a word-for-word transliterations of the interview.

Through this book, we are trying to capture the essence of Sister Shivani's thoughts and understanding of Happiness and its various dimensions.

Note to the Reader

Dear Reader,

This book looks at, probes into, questions, gets baffled by, embraces and ultimately substantiates the pursuit of happiness. In its tracing of the conversation between Suresh Oberoi, and Sister Shivani, Here, in the unpredictability and certainties of questions, more questions and answers emerge ideas of the self, choices, conditioning, perceptions, actions, karmas, belief systems, experiences... these together hold for us the experience (and the mystery) that we understand and feel as happiness.

At the core of the 'happiness' conversation is the comprehension and acceptance of the self. *Spirituality is not about doing things or becoming someone – it is just about being who we truly are.* This thought reverberates through the book, in its recalling of incidents, interactions and own experiences. You, the reader, will be able to find yourself in many of these situations that bring to the fore the eternal human conflicts that have held us in thrall since the beginning of life.

Because of the very reason that the conversation includes you in a real sense, the book that you are holding at this moment is expected to have an empowering effect. So that you take charge of your life and awaken to your pure and perfect inner self. This will happen because you will begin to unravel your own subconscious beliefs and perceptions that control your thoughts, feelings and actions.

Here, then, is the beginning of self-transformation and the first steps toward happiness.

Om Shanti!

BOOK 1
'CHOOSING HAPPINESS'

It is the Choice I Make

There is a time to bid goodbye to the old and the ordinary, and to awaken the beauty within. That time is now. It is time to wake up and take charge of life, and rethink refreshingly. Indeed, it is time to awaken with Brahma Kumaris.

Om Shanti!

Suresh Oberoi: What is the meaning of happiness?

Sister Shivani: Happiness is the one thing in life that everyone is looking for, irrespective of what we are doing, what relationships we have established, what we are trying to achieve, and so on. If we think about life, clearly all of us are looking for happiness.

SO: We are looking for happiness as you said. But what is it through which we are looking for it?

SS: We do it through different means—it could be through possessions, through property, through relationships, through achievements, through good health. Like, if you ask someone what they want in life, they often say 'success'. Why they want success is primarily because it makes them happy. You ask someone why they want to buy a particular thing. The most likely response is that it makes them happy or maybe it makes the family happy. Again you ask someone what they get out of a relationship? Yet again, the response is often Happiness. So, finally everyone is looking for that one word—HAPPINESS.

SO: But is happiness limited or unlimited? It is limited, isn't it?
SS: It is. In fact, I don't even know whether it's there.

SO: So it is momentary—like a child who plays with a toy and breaks it, and then wants to try another one, then another one, and so on. So what are we looking for actually? If we are looking for happiness, shouldn't it be something concrete and permanent?
SS: It should be permanent, that's most important. If happiness is something that I like, if it's something that I desire, and if comes naturally to me, then it won't be dependent on anything else outside. If it's dependent on something, then it can never be constant.

Simply put, if you are looking for it outside somewhere, then you are dependent on that thing and the feeling won't sustain. Let's say I feel good if the weather is pleasant; my feeling good is then dependent on the weather.

SO: Sure! But what I want to understand is that how can

one have happiness without desires and dependency?

SS: That's probably one of the oldest belief systems we have allowed ourselves to live by—the belief that happiness is to be got from the outside, whether it's from achievements or from people or from what we are. 'I am doing this so that I will feel happy',", is always the equation. When it's done, and done in the right way, I will feel happy. So, the dependency is on the act being performed in the right manner. Right from when a child is conditioned by the parents to make the parents feel good when the child gets good marks, when the child performs well, when the child looks good.

Slowly a child is conditioned to believe that if my parents feel happy then I will feel happy, and if my parents are not happy then how can I be happy?

SO: Can you share some easier way or the right way whereby we can understand the meaning of happiness and understand how to achieve it without dependency?

SS: First and foremost, let's try and see on what it is dependent. The simplest dependency that we experience on a daily basis is on objects. I'll feel happy when I buy a new car; I'll feel happy when I buy new property; I am happy when I go shopping.

SO: But what is wrong in this? Isn't this natural?

SS: What is more important—'Is it true?' Are these dependencies actually making us happy?

SO: Honestly speaking, I will feel happy if I bought a new car.

SS: Of course you will, but is it the car which is giving you that happiness, which you are looking for.

I will feel happy when I have a new car... which means, if I don't, then it's a question mark. This also means that 10 days down the line if the car gets a little scratch or a little bump, my happiness is again going to get affected because I have conditioned myself into believing that it is the car which is giving me happiness. Now that is not true. You buy a new car—the car could be of X amount, or it could be ten times the X amount; in fact, it could be the most expensive car in the world. You sit in the car and it very comfortable. So who is experiencing the comfort? It's the body. It's got excellent seats, a great music system and a very powerful AC. There is complete physical comfort. I am comfortable sitting in the car and so I tell myself that I am feeling good. And just at that time I get a phone call saying something unpleasant has happened at home. Will I still be happy?

SO: No.
SS: But I am still comfortable. The car is still there and I am still in the car. The car was designed to give me physical comfort and it will give me physical comfort irrespective of any other life event that I encounter.

SO: So, you mean to say that happiness and comfort are two different things?
SS: Anything that is physical is designed to give me physical comfort. The chair I am sitting on is physical and giving me physical comfort, but I tell myself that this gives me happiness.

SO: Is this a wrong belief that we have?

SS: It's just that we were conditioned to think like this right from childhood. We have grown up with it. But now we need to question our belief system.

SO: When we were children our parents would buy something for us, saying 'we'll buy this for him and make the child happy', or would take us for a picnic to make us feel 'happy'. So that is the way we got conditioned.

SS: Absolutely. Now I have the best bungalow and the best car, and I have all possessions I could have dreamed of at home; I have every gadget that I wanted. Then why am I still looking for happiness? Shouldn't the search have ended because the objects are all there at home? Name it and I have it all. But I seem to be still searching for that feeling, which means the gadgets are not able to give it to me. What I have got from the gadgets is a comfortable life.

SO: In the context of the car that you mentioned, the comfort is also no more there when the phone call says that something unpleasant has happened at home. So, where is the comfort here?

SS: Picture yourself sitting in the car, your back straight, and your legs positioned comfortably. It is the mind that has suddenly created the pain because of the new information. When the mind gets uncomfortable, it is mind over matter. When the mind is in pain, physical comfort is immaterial. The body is comfortable—but 'I' am uncomfortable at that moment.

I am looking for happiness. So, at that moment the

physical comfort does not matter. It could be the other way round too. I may be uncomfortable physically, I may just be sitting cross-legged on the floor, but internally I feel bliss, and so I am very comfortable.

SO: How does one get there?
SS: One gets there by understanding that physical comfort is separate from emotional comfort. I was not able to experience internal comfort—the internal stability that we call happiness, but I thought that if I am physically comfortable, then that means I will be happy. Today, we have started to buy happiness If I buy this, this and this... the list is never-ending—I will be happy. This doesn't mean that we don't buy those things, rather let's not associate them with our being happy. I generally buy a thing because it's useful, it's comfortable or it's productive. But is it happiness? No!

At least I know why I am buying something; and I don't tell my mind that when I buy this I will be happy. If I associate material things with happiness then I am postponing my happiness and putting a new condition to it. Let's suppose that I am building a new house and I tell myself that when this house is built and I shift there, then I will be happy. This could mean after a year or after two years.

So, again I am postponing my happiness until a future time. Think of a child—we look at the child in school and say that childhood is the best phase of life, but the child looks at the grownups around him and thinks they are so lucky, for they don't have to do homework or give an exam. He wishes to be in their place. The child is looking to be out of school so that he can be happy. He feels he will be very happy when he goes to a college. Then, when he gets into a college the thought is redefined. He feels he will be very happy when he gets a job, is married and has a family. But soon, he feels that he will be very happy when his children are settled. Few years down the line, the children are settled and everything is fine. What is the thought now? He feels he will be very happy when he retires. So, when will he actually be happy? He postponed his happiness to a different stage of life and every time there was a new blank to fill in. We are stuck in a vicious circle where we tell ourselves: when *this happens, I will be happy.*

SO: How distressing!
SS: True! And that's why we are not happy.

SO: We see so many people who are rich; they have helicopters, private airplanes, their own boats, everything. They still wander from temple to temple, from one guru to another. Finally, what are they seeking? How does one put an end to this search?
SS: First, by understanding that it is separate and second, by understanding that it is my internal creation and I can create it irrespective of everything else. I buy a car and then I say I am happy. The car is a physical object with no feelings or emotions. Obviously the car is not giving me happiness. So, what is? I create the thought: 'Wow! I bought a car. I finally bought what I wanted.' These are positive thoughts.

It is the same with say a woman with a new jewellery set. Is it the jewellery set that is giving her happiness? Or it is she who is creating the positive thought of possessing that set, which she thinks is giving her happiness?

SO: But don't you think that the positive thought cannot be created minus the jewellery set?

SS: Yeah! This means I need an object as a stimulus to create a response. So it's the object, and the object can be anything, like the jewellery set. I look at the object and I create a thought within.

So when we acquire the object, our natural response is 'This is a lovely piece of jewellery that I have just got.' Now who created this thought?

SO: That's a tricky question to answer. I create the thought or was it created because of the object?

SS: A physical piece of jewellery does not have thoughts and feelings. I look at it and I create a thought—'I have bought such a lovely piece of jewellery!' If 10 minutes later somebody walks into the room and says this is not looking nice on you or says this is fake, then what? Now who is creating the response? If the stimulus was creating the response then the stimulus will keep on creating the same response, irrespective of a change in situation. Further, if I show the same piece of jewellery to 10 people, will all of them create the same thoughts? For someone it's too loud—I can't wear this, I don't like this at all; for another it could be—I am sorry, I don't like jewellery at all; it could also be—I really want this or how sad that I can't afford this. The piece of jewellery is the same.

SO: My reaction to the piece is my choice.

SS: It is my thought.

SO: I am reacting, which means I am creating. I am creating either happiness or unhappiness.

SS: So we could create thoughts of pleasure or thoughts of jealousy or hurt with the same object of jewellery. The stimulus is the same, the object is the same. If the object had to create the thought, it would create the same thought in everyone.

If the object—whether a car, a piece of jewellery, or a lovely garden—is what is creating the thought, then it should create the same thought in every person. Look at this greenery. You may think how lovely it is to be with nature, while another person may just overlook it while walking and not even realize.

These are different responses to the same stimulus. The response is the choice of the creator and I am the creator.

SO: I am the creator and I am creating unhappiness or happiness. Sister Shivani, many of my thoughts and questions have been answered by this. But how does one do without a stimulus?

SS: By understanding that I am creating the thought. We were not aware that we are the creators. We tend to believe that thoughts come to us because of something outside. Let's suppose that you say something which according to me is a little rude, and I get hurt. I do not even think that I am creating that feeling of being hurt. I very conveniently say— You hurt me. I think it is all coming from outside. Then I say that you need to talk nicely to me for me to feel better. You better apologize because once you do that, I am going to feel better. This is dependency.

SO: Then he would say I never meant that.
SS: But you hurt me. We can just go on and on. I am hurt because of you ... I am angry because of you ... I am upset because of you ... I am jealous because of you ... I am happy because of you.

SO: If everything is happening because of others around, it means I am not taking responsibility of myself.
SS: No responsibility and no control! How helpless are we if we are always dependent on anything external.

SO: Isn't that a weakness?
SS: But isn't that the way we are living our lives? The minute we understand that this is an illusion, that they are not controlling us, and we are not dependent on them, we have a choice of what we create. This is independence. That's why the first thing that spirituality gives us is freedom. It liberates us. We are liberated from all the dependencies, everything we thought we were dependent on and postponed your happiness. We just postponed it, convincing ourselves that we could not be happy till we had what we wanted.

SO: It is very difficult to understand how I can be happy without what I want?
SS: We talked about objects, but what about achievements? 'I wanted to achieve this particular goal but I haven't reached there, so how can I be happy?' We have been brought up to believe that only those who achieve what they want

12

will be happy This is what we were taught when we were children.

SO: I always thought that it was very natural to be that way. If I fail to get a job three times in a row, then I feel depressed, and it's very normal. I used to think like that.
SS: I thought that my happiness was dependent on getting the job. I thought it was normal and that's why getting upset was a normal reaction too. Getting tensed is normal, to worry is normal, to fear is normal, to feel sad is normal, but to feel happy doesn't come so easily to us. Problems will come, challenges will be there, but to despair or to deal with them is our choice.

Because everything else is outside.

SO: But that outside is also disturbing me inside.
SS: That's the choice. Does it disturb everyone in the same manner? Faced with failure, someone could go into depression, someone else could commit suicide, and yet another one would say 'Okay, I'm doing it again,' and be successful the next time. This is same failure, but different responses.

That's why my thoughts and feelings are in my hand. Just this one mechanism will change the way I live my life.

SO: But isn't it too quick? Between the moment when something happens and when you react, there is hardly any time to tell oneself that 'Look, this is a thought and it is just something outside and not inside.' Where is the time for me to control my reaction?
SS: That's why we are living our lives in an automated mode.

You know it's like how a machine functions. What's the difference between a machine and a human being?

A machine has no choice—we put it on and off and then on and off. It is dependent on the person who is using it. You press the button and it's on, press the button again and it's off. Human beings, have a choice. Someone comes and says something to me—they press a button; if I am a machine I will say 'obviously I will get angry.' What is obvious about it? Obvious is only for a machine because it is made to work automatically.

SO: But everybody is living in that automated mode except for the saints and a few others.
SS: No, it's not about saints. It's just about being aware that we are human beings. People are pressing the button but we have a choice.

SO: Do say something about the meditation you do every day. Probably because of this practice you have been able to understand the difference between what is happening outside and what you are creating inside. How can one meditate like you? People usually think that meditation is about sitting in a corner and not thinking. It's so difficult for us to not think for a moment. Can you make this a little easy for us?
SS: Let me tell you a very simple thing: meditation is not about stopping the thinking process, rather it is to be aware of what I am thinking and to choose what I am going to be thinking.

SO: To be aware of what I am thinking...
SS: Yes, like we are aware of what we are speaking.

SO: I am not aware.
SS: You are not speaking in an automated mode. You choose what to speak, you choose your actions—when to sit, when to get up, when to walk, when to sleep. We are choosing our actions, our words. Of course, sometimes the thoughts come so fast that we feel even the words are automated, and we say 'I didn't mean to say that.' So, a step further will be to become aware of what I am thinking, to choose our thoughts and thereby choose our responses. It's a simple exercise we begin every morning and can do it any time during the day – just watch your thoughts.

Relax and reflect on these thoughts:
What am I thinking right now: it could be about work, about family, about friends, about myself. Let me look at my thoughts ... Look at myself during the whole day: driving to work, reaching my desk, interacting with people ... I am doing everything but I am choosing what to do and I am choosing how to be while I am doing it ... I have a choice how to feel while I am doing everything I am doing outside... Situations, targets, goals, people – they are all external... Let me look at myself: how I think, how I feel, and then how I respond... It's my choice... I am the creator of my response.

MANTRAS FOR HAPPINESS UNLIMITED

- Happiness is not dependent on physical objects.

- Objects, possessions, gadgets, etc., are designed to give us comfort.

- Physical comfort is different from emotional comfort.

- Happiness is our internal creation and can be created irrespective of external comforts.

- We use objects as a stimulus to create a response, but the response is our choice. Different people create different responses using the same stimulus.

- Problems will come, challenges will be there, but to despair or deal with them is our choice.

To Create the Thought, to Embrace the Journey

SO: We have been talking about dependency in happiness—how we are dependent on so many things for happiness. Sister Shivani, you say it is "I" who create happiness, "I" who create sadness. It's finally "I" who is responsible. Yet, it's very difficult to be happy when you have not achieved something in life.

SS: There are two dynamics here: one, if I achieve this then I will be happy, and another, I will be happy while achieving this. It's like we are on a journey, say from X to Y, and Y is the destination whether we are going by road, by train, or by air. When we start on the journey, others wish us a safe journey, not 'reach your destination anyways'. It's not only reaching the destination that matters, it's the quality of the journey that counts.

SO: That's how many of us think that we have to reach our destination by hook or by crook.

SS: Okay, let's look at it this way. I have set a goal for myself, whether it's for marks as a student, for a professional position in my organization, or it could be in my relationships. In any case, we are not going to be able to lead our lives without goals, because without goals we will become passive. I wouldn't know where I am heading. Now, the other thing that I do is tell myself that I will be happy when I reach the goal. The goal may take six months or six years. So I start moving to, say, reach this particular position in my organization in the coming two years. Now I start my journey. It is about the way I work, the way I am with my colleagues, the way I am performing. Continuously, at the back of my mind I believe that when I reach there I will be happy. Now if there is a little lapse in the way I am working, if people around me are uncooperative, if there are certain obstacles coming in the way, what will happen to me?

SO: I will not be happy.

SS: Because I will create stress, I will create anxiety. Why? Because people are coming in the way of my happiness. I see them as obstacles not just in my goal, but also in my happiness. Now suppose that I am going to walk from here to there and my mind says happiness is there. I start walking. While I am walking you are in the way, and because you are in the way I see you as someone in the way of my happiness. I will do anything to get you out of the way. If you are just a junior I will shout at you and order you to work fast. If you are a colleague and I think you are a threat to me in my reaching the goal, I can plot anything against you to get you out of the way. I may even compromise on my values. Suppose during my journey you tell me that if I am honest I'll have to stop here for one week, but if I tell a lie I can go there faster. Now, many of us wouldn't even think twice before using the other method. I might end up telling a lie and that's where I will compromise on my values and principles during my journey. I have begun to think that my values and principles are delaying my process of attaining my happiness.

SO: But if you are going to get happiness, how does it matter if you were to lie?
SS: At this moment we are still on the journey; we haven't reached the destination yet. While on the journey, I am creating anger and stress, and I am compromising on my values and principles. So, I am creating negative emotions in the course of my journey. For six months I create anxiety and stress, which in turn can disturb my relationships and create issues with people at work. My inner state of mind will be in an upheaval, and eventually it will start affecting my physical health. Finally, after six months when I reach my goal, how will I feel?

SO: Don't you think you will be happy?
SS: If I have created all these negative emotions on the way... I have experienced and have also transmitted the same emotions to everyone around me; all this happened on the journey. It's like I have fallen down, hurt myself,

and then reached there. By the time I reached there, I am totally in pain. But because I have reached there I am very happy. Now my conditioning says happiness is dependent on achievement.

SO: You want to achieve further. The driving force becomes "achieve–achieve–achieve", and you are caught up in its pursuit. You go home and say "oh, I'm so sorry I have been behaving like this, coming home late at night, troubling you, but I have to achieve the target".
SS: So, if for example you set a six-month goal, for the whole of six months you are allowing yourself to get bruised and hurt emotionally.

SO: This means we are not just postponing happiness, we are actually creating unhappiness all the way. And this is going to multiply.
SS: Exactly. In the first six months, to reach (A) I was bruised because I created negative emotions around me, hurt people, lost my temper, whatever. By the time I reach (A), my emotional strength has already become weaker. During the next journey from (A) to (B), my strength is already weakened. It is the same environment, the same people, the same situations, but the weak emotional strength means I am going to get bruised further.

SO: Is it emotional strength?
SS: My power to face situations. I will get hurt more easily, I will react, I will get irritated.

SO: Don't you think all these things also make you physically weak?

SS: It's going to have an effect on the body, but when we are young we don't feel the impact. So we think it is absolutely fine, this is natural, this is the way to live. It's only later that we start showing symptoms of hypertension, diabetes and similar troubles. Since we accept stress as a part of our lives we also accept the physical symptoms as inevitable.

SO: I still can't understand how someone can be happy without achieving his goal. He comes home as a failure, and with so many problems.

SS: Let's say I am looking for a job and I have been trying for the last six months. I am not getting a job and I am very demotivated and upset. As a friend, what would you say to me?

SO: Don't worry, it happens. One day you will get it. Meanwhile please let me know if I can be of help.

SS: If I say how can I not be worried, I haven't got a job for the last six months, what are you going to say to me?

SO: By worrying will you get it?

SS: So, just let's say this to ourselves: by worrying will I get it?

SO: That is very easily said…

SS: But that's the solution. The more I worry, the weaker my mind becomes; it starts to show in my body language; I lose my enthusiasm and I get thoughts like how will I get a job? To get a job I need confidence, I need to be enthusiastic, I need to be ready to face the challenges the new job offers. It's not about what has happened, it's about what I need to do now—how does my state of being have to be. I have to take care of that, else I am trapped in the vicious cycle of negativity. Who is going to employ a person who is demotivated and has given up on life? Who do you think will hire a person who has lost his internal strength and tolerance, who is unable to get along with people, and is not able to create team spirit? Who is going to hire a candidate like that? So, whatever the situation may be and however challenging it may be, I am not going to get the solution unless I take care of myself. My business is not doing well and so it is natural for me to worry, but if I worry I will still not be able to do well. If I want to do well outside, I will have to be well within. But what is most important is: even if I don't do well, at least I can take care of myself.

SO: I had a guru who told me about a man who was undergoing a prolonged struggle due to a court case. At the same time he was also worried about his wife, who was very sick. Finally, after about 15 years he won the court case and his wife too recovered. But then he himself fell sick and died. Despite knowing of this humbling tale, why is it so difficult for me to understand what you are telling me right now?
SS: It's about priorities in life. What are my responsibilities in life? Normally I will count my family, my job, my work, my home, my friends, my relatives, my society, my relationships, my country...

We can take responsibility of our family and move on to the entire world, but not our own responsibility. Let's say we are a family of five and four of them are not well. I want to take the responsibility of taking care of them, of healing them, but I will only be able to do that if I am healthy myself. This is about physical health. Now you apply the same equation to emotional health; I want to take care of my children, my wife, my husband, my parents; I want to ensure that they are happy ... but I am in pain.

SO: I even get sad when they are not able to do well in class. I wanted them to become swimming champions, tennis players, and so on.
SS: Why do you want to do all that? Just so that they will be happy! Finally, I want everyone around me to be happy.

SO: And if they are happy, I will be happy.
SS: I thought I would take care of everything and then they will be happy; and when they are happy, then I will be happy. Spirituality teaches us that when I am happy and I am able to take care of them, then they will also be happy.

SO: So when I am happy, I am also spreading my happy emotions around. Wherever I go I am alive with happiness and I make other people happy too.
SS: Because you make them stronger. Let's see, what is happiness? Happiness is an internal strength. It does not mean excitement, I am not going to be jumping and dancing the whole day. I have lost my job and I am not excited about it.

23

SO: Happiness is strength... I am not able to understand this.

SS: See, at any given point in time, there can only be one thought in the mind. One thought possesses one quality. That one quality could be either the right quality or the not-so-right quality. If I am creating a pure, powerful and positive thought, then it is the right quality. If I am creating a negative thought, an unpleasant thought, a thought of anxiety, pain and worry, it's a wrong thought. If it's the right thought I feel good; if it's not the right thought I feel low. If it's the right thought, then I feel good and that is stability. If it is not the right thought, I feel low and that is weakness.

SO: So, stability is strength.

SS: If you are stable, you are strong. This strength will then shape the way you respond to situations. Like, you said, I want my child to have good marks. Okay, I want my child to have good marks but it is not necessary that this will happen every time. When he fails to get the marks I expect him to get or the marks he is capable of getting, what is my state of mind? I am upset. Is that good for me? No. Is that good for my child? No. Then why am I creating it? The marks did not create my feelings, rather I was the creator of what I felt.

SO: But I would have thought it was just normal to be upset and feel sad.

SS: Once I get upset, my child also gets upset. My child gets demotivated and I expect him to do well in that demotivated state of mind. The energy that i am giving to those around

24

me is not positive, and that's why I am not fulfilling my responsibility in the right way. When my child gets less marks, my responsibility should be to first take charge of my mind; I have to remain composed so that I don't react immediately by shouting at him. Next, my responsibility is to take care of his state of mind, and finally I carefully explain to him that he needs to study responsibly and get good marks the next time.

SO: So what we usually end up offering our child is the opposite. We deplete his energy, lower his self-esteem, and make him feel small. I think that's why suicides among children are prevalent today.

SS: A big reason why a child commits suicide is that he is not able to face his parents after the failure. It is not because he failed; it is because he doesn't want to see his parents unhappy and he holds himself responsible for their unhappiness. The parents had conditioned and pressured him throughout the year that they would be happy only when he succeeded.

SO: I thought it was my responsibility to see to it that my child achieved his goal—whether in studies, sports, or whatever else. I realize that I have been doing just the opposite.

SS: Every individual's life is based on four aspects: physical, intellectual, emotional and spiritual. It is about my physical health, my intellectual development, my emotional state of being and my spiritual health. If I want to be successful in life and if I want my children to be successful in life—successful in the whole sense, then all the four aspects need to be equally balanced. When I consider my responsibilities toward my child, I take into account his academic performance and extracurricular performance, and I take care of his physical health. My child should get the best home, the best food, the best exercise and so on. With regard to his social well-being, I want him to have good friends and indulge in extracurricular activities. But how is my child feeling inside? We are not really considering and taking care of that aspect. Physically and academically he may be doing very well, but the constant pressure, the constant comparison with other people, and the constant criticism that he gets from his parents are actually depleting his emotional strength. So I have to ask myself whether I am fulfilling my responsibility. Tomorrow he could grow up to be a good doctor or a senior lawyer, and be physically very strong, but if he is emotionally not strong, will he be a good human being? And if he is not a good human being, a pure and powerful being, will he really be happy?

SO: What happens if he is emotionally not very strong?
SS: If I am a good doctor, technically I am good. But if I am not emotionally strong, then I will get irritated very easily, I will react easily, I will not empathize with my patients and my colleagues. I will not get along with people because I am intolerant. Can I still call myself a good doctor?

While we were growing up they only taught us how to read, how to write, how to speak. No one taught us how to think.

SO: But that's what happens, Sister Shivani. We knew

only about IQ; EQ came into the picture much later.

SS: There is no doubt that your IQ is important, but so is your emotional strength. The emotionally strong person can handle all struggles and challenges of life. With a strong IQ we need emotional strength to achieve success.

SO: When I was, growing up I remember that, adults often slapped children to teach them, even at schools. If they scored less marks, they felt sacred to share those marks at home.

SS: Right. So we need to ask ourselves whether we are fulfilling all our responsibilities suitably. It is not enough to fulfil one responsibility by getting them to perform well. What about my second responsibility of making the child a strong human being? Life is going to present a lot of challenges. Today your child has passed with the highest marks and come first in class, but will his marks help him face all the challenges in life?

SO: Maybe emotionally he is so weak that he will not be able to compete with other things in life.

SS: Exactly. If he has to face even a small failure, he will not be able to cope up. What if he has to work with people with whom he cannot adjust? We did not take care of that aspect. Why? The prime reason is that we had not taken care of that aspect in our own lives. We ignored the importance of being emotionally healthy. We thought our responsibility is to take care of everything external, whether in our lives or the lives of those for whom we were responsible.

SO: Most men feel that their responsibility is to earn money and when they do that their job is done.

SS: The husband feels he has fulfilled all the needs of the family. Now if he has given them all of this, then they should be happy because happiness is supposed to be coming from outside.

SO: We give them good toys, good clothes, good food, etc.; we have done our duty. Now if they don't study, that's their problem. We easily put it to *sanskaras*, their school, or peer pressure. We keep on blaming other people.

SS: Because you are not ready to take that responsibility. It's easy to earn and to send your child to the best school, to give him the best food and the best home, and the best of everything, but it's a huge challenge to make your child emotionally strong.

SO: The most important thing I have to realize is that first I have to be emotionally strong. Let us do a little meditation here Sister Shivani.

SS: So it's time to do that now. While taking care of our children we always need to remember, we can send our child to the best school without having gone to school ourselves. We can ensure that our children eat well, even if we sleep empty stomach. But it is not possible to make our children happy without being happy ourselves. You cannot make your child emotionally strong without being emotionally strong yourself, so that's where the responsibility comes—to find it first in yourself.

SS: Relax and reflect on these thoughts:

Let us sit back and look at the journey of our life... aims, objectives, achievements ... milestones to cover ... that is my journey ... Let me look at myself on the journey ... the traveller with the changed consciousness... Happiness is not at the destination ... happiness is my state of being on the journey. I am happy ... stable ... in control ... powerful while I am on the journey... There are obstacles on the way ... but my first responsibility is to take care of my state of being ... of the way I respond ... This is my responsibility. Om Shanti!

MANTRAS FOR HAPPINESS UNLIMITED

- Happiness is a state of being created while working towards the goal, not a feeling to be experienced after achieving the goal.

- If we believe that happiness is experienced after achievement, then we create stress, anger and fear while trying to achieve it. Thus we ultimately do not experience happiness.

- Before I take responsibility of those around me, I need to take responsibility for my own thinking and feelings. When I am happy and take care of others, then they will be happy.

- You cannot make your child emotionally strong without being emotionally strong yourself.

First, I Will Take Care of Myself

SO: I have been speaking to a few friends and they mentioned something called the u-stress—meaning good stress. They say we need that kind of stress and tension. One of my friend's claims that he actually waits till he is stressed and time is less, because then he works best. How should one understand that?

SS: It's a belief system. It is something that we are hearing everywhere around us—that unless there is stress I will not perform; if there is no stress I will become passive and laidback. They call it the drive to perform, to achieve. So we need to ask ourselves: is it really true? For that I need to ask myself what is this stress and how do I feel when I experience it. Imagine that I suddenly have a problem in my knee and it starts paining. I am still walking but is it the same as I was walking before, when everything was fine?

SO: No, there is pain now.

SS: Naturally it's to going to be a little uncomfortable. However, I say this is okay, or even accept it as a natural part of ageing. I keep walking and because I am not treating it or taking care of it, the pain is constantly there and at times it aggravates. I am still managing my life, though. Now, suddenly I have to run because of some reason. Will I be able to run with that pain? I will not be able to. It's the same with stress. Stress is in my mind; it is a little pain in the way I feel. How do I feel when I experience stress? Even if I am not able to check myself at the emotional level, let's just check the physical or bodily parameters—my heartbeat increases and so does my pulse rate, at times my mouth goes dry, I start getting a very uncomfortable feeling in the stomach, my head feels heavy, and so on. This is when the effect of the mind has already taken a toll on the body, and it is a much later stage. Some students fall ill on the day of their exams, with fever or nausea. Some people start sweating or their mouth goes dry before a public speech. This is the effect of the mind on the body.

SO: But I thought it was normal. The first time I was facing a camera, my mouth and lips had all gone dry.
SS: Did you perform better?

SO: No, it was very bad.
SS: Let's say a child has to sit for an exam. Exam is a target and a pressure. If he creates anxiety, does he perform better? I remember when we used to give our exams and come back and evaluate our own performance, we would point out places where we knew the answer but made mistakes. We referred

31

to these as careless mistakes. What is a careless mistake? I know the answer but I have written something else. And why have I done it? Because there is no clarity, which is a state brought about by the presence of anxiety.

It's not carelessness. It has happened because I did not take care of my mind. So there is no clarity in thinking, decision-making power is affected, performance gets affected, my hands tremble, and my speed of writing slows down. I may even say that I didn't finish my exam.

SS: SO: So why do people say that they work best when they are stressed and tensed, and when the deadline is looming on their heads?

SS: Deadline means there is a target and target could be a pressure. Target means I have to do this by so and so time. If you remove that target I may take six days to complete the same task. The minute you set a target, I start working faster. Now, while I am working faster, what will happen if I start creating thoughts along these lines—how will I finish it by tomorrow evening; if I don't finish it by tomorrow evening, what will the consequence be? Will I be thrown out of my job? Will my boss get angry with me? What if someone else finishes it before I do? Does that mean they will have a better chance for a promotion or a raise? If this happens, my career is finished! I am still performing, I am still working, but what is going on in the mind? What is going on in the mind is stress; negativity is the stress because it is creating an uncomfortable feeling. The target is fine. Two people are given the same target: they have to finish this job by tomorrow evening, both are set to achieve it and they will. This means both will reach the destination but the journey will be different for each of them. One will think 'yes, I have to achieve this by tomorrow evening, I will have nothing else but this work on my mind, and I am going to do this'. The second person will worry 'what if something happens', or 'what if I don't achieve this'. So, one has reached the destination with stability, and the other has done the same by creating stress. The end result is externally the same, for both have performed, but internally the other person is totally fatigued. This other person will conveniently put blame on the pressure, and not realise that it is his own creation in the face of pressure.

Stress in science has a simple formula:

$$stress = pressure \div resilience$$

Pressure, the numerator here, includes what's coming from outside—targets, exams, relationships, situations, traffic jams, deadlines, etc. Resilience is my inner strength to face that pressure. Consider the simple metal sheets used in industrial applications. Different metal sheets are subjected to the same amount of pressure, but the stress factor of every metal is different because every metal sheet's power to face that pressure is different.

Now in the formula *stress = pressure ÷ resilience*, we have conveniently ignored the denominator and embraced the conditioning of stress = *pressure*.

It's ignored, because I am not ready to take responsibility for my inner strength. Hence, for me stress = pressure. If I have an exam, obviously I will get tensed. If my boss is very tough, obviously it is going to be a challenge for me because stress = *pressure*.

SO: Do you think people like to be stressed? Why do we accept it easily?
SS: When I am not able to tackle it, I just say it's natural or inevitable.

SO: You mean to say it takes effort to not be stressed and be happy in the situation?
SS: Yes! Suppose you say something to me that is not pleasant. To get hurt is so easy...

SO: Even at my age, I tend to think it's so natural to blame others for how we feel.
SS: The weather changes. It's summer today, a couple months later it will be winter. The weather changes and it gets chilly. Do you say it's natural to fall ill since the weather has changed? No! You open the cupboard and take out the woollens and protect yourself.

We don't keep blaming the weather, do we? We protect ourselves. Things are going to happen outside but because we have not learnt the mechanism of how to protect ourselves, we say it is natural to fall ill. It's natural to get hurt, to get stressed, that's what we say.

Spirituality focuses on the denominator, that is resilience. The pressure or the situation is not in my control. So the numerator is not in my control. In any situation we can attribute 10% to the numerator, but the remaining 90% depends on my power to cope. Because if there is no pressure, then there will be no stress, so we give 10% responsibility to the pressure. The remaining 90% is about the extent I take charge of how I am going to handle that pressure.

SO: So, how I react to something is 90%. Somebody just hits my car—if it's an old car, I don't really get that upset; but if it's a brand new one, I react. What do you say?
SS: How you react is your choice. Someone has hit your car—the situation was not in your control. Now, you have two ways to respond: 1) Get out of the car, create a scene, shout at him, hit him, abuse him, have him respond in the same manner, and have ten more people in the scene, or 2) wish him good morning and a nice day.

SO: And the other choice is to just smile and say it's okay. In any case your car is insured.
SS: Yes! More important is the insurance of the mind. You claim insurance and your car is repaired. But for the damage that gets done inside you every time a situation arises, where is the insurance for that and where are the repairs?

SO: I am more concerned that my car is damaged.
SS: The car is more important than my happiness on my responsibility list, because I thought the car was my source of happiness. Only when I make my state of being as my priority will I start taking care of myself. First check if you are okay, then check if everything outside of you is okay.

SO: If you don't help yourself, how can you help others?

But isn't this being a bit selfish?

SS: If I don't take care of myself, can I help you? All my time and energy is spent in taking care of other people. What's the result? Today I am under stress, and so are my children. Earlier, depression was something that affected people when they were 60 and above; today we have school children with so many issues and are frequenting counsellors and psychiatrists. If we were fulfilling our responsibilities, this wouldn't be the result.

SO: We often say that the teachers are irresponsible, the politicians are irresponsible, but thinking inwards I am the most irresponsible person especially by not being responsible for myself.

SS: First I have to be responsible. The ability to respond is *responsibility*. My ability to respond in every situation is *response + ability = responsibility.*

Imagine the irony of life—we are always trying to control things that are not in our control, while ignoring the one thing that is in our control. We say, 'oh, my mind is not in my control', but that is the only thing that is in one's control. Going back to the matter of two cars bumping into each other—if you suggest to people that you can just say "okay, never mind" and drive away, they might not agree. They strongly feel that it is important to get out of the car and shout at the one who made the mistake. You try and explain to them that it will be damaging for them, that is they will be hurting themselves.. They will say but what about making the other person realise their mistake.

SO: So that he won't repeat the mistake again. I am doing him a favour.

SS: You see I am more interested in teaching others rather than taking care of myself. Whether it's a small situation or a big one, I have a choice of how I am going to respond. Let me just sit back and be aware in every situation. If I just say it's okay and drive on, how do I feel on that day?

SO: I would feel nice about it.

SS: Because you have conserved energy and conquered your own weakness. So it is something that has to be experimented with.

SO: The other day I was going to the airport and somebody banged my car. My driver was just about to get out and fight, but I asked him to keep quiet, close the door and ignore the other person. I felt nice about it. Right now, conversing with you, I realize I felt nice because I kind of conquered my weakness that has been there for years and years.

SS: Also, you had the right thoughts at that moment, so you felt better. If you create the thought that "it's okay, it's just an accident, move on now", it's a positive thought. It's a good feeling. But if I have thoughts like—why didn't he look where he was driving; he should have been driving carefully; who gives them their driving license; they think they own the road—how are you going to feel after that? The thoughts you have will determine your feelings. Then, after all this we reach our destination, maybe we were headed to our workplace.

SO: And for how long will this kind of mood and the agitation remain?

SS: Let's say I have to drive for about half-an-hour to work. So, the mood will stay with me for about half-an-hour. However, the unfortunate part is, within the next half an hour there will be another situation. By that time my emotional immunity system is already low and the chances of me reacting has increased. Next I reach my office and me receptionist is not there on her desk… She has not come to office on time. Now yet another situation confronts me. I go to my desk and see that the office boy has not cleaned my table properly. One more situation. My junior has not completed his work, which was supposed to be there on my desk at 10 o'clock in the morning. So, situation after situation unfolds, and I keep reacting. Every time I justify my reaction by saying it is because of…

SO: …this, this, this. I am right, I didn't do anything but this happened, and it is natural.

SS: If you react, you are wasting and depleting your energy; you are reducing your emotional strength. When you encounter the next situation you will be weaker than before.

SO: Over a period of time it also becomes a habit. Then you get high blood pressure and heart problems start and so on. It takes a toll on our health.

SS: Today we say high blood pressure is natural because the stress is natural, and the by-product of this stress will also be natural. So everything that was unnatural gets labelled as natural. And then we say we want happiness.

SO: Tell me, what is the meaning of unlimited?
SS: That which is not dependent on any limited object, people or situation. It's a state of being that is unlimited, unconditional, and independent. It is free of dependencies and, therefore, free of the fear of failure. Whenever there is dependency on someone or something, the second thought instantly will be of fear. What if I don't get it? I have immediately created fear and as I create fear, the happiness is gone. You will find people fearing happiness too—when everyone in the house is happy, someone will say "don't be so happy, you never know what's going to happen next." They are so fearful that they are scared to be happy today.

SO: Everything is temporary.
SS: Because it's all dependent on situations. Today the situation is favourable, so you are happy, but you don't know what the next situation is going to be. But, if your happiness is independent of situations, then you can be happy 24 x 7.

SO: You think we can be happy 24 x 7?
SS: It's possible and we can do it, but first we have to take care of ourselves and take self-responsibility. But if it depends on outside factors then it is occasional. The more the situations become challenging; the more people's behaviours become unpredictable. It becomes a struggle and that is why we start accepting stress as natural, whereas it is happiness that is natural.

SO: Sister Shivani, thank you so much for explaining how stress is not natural – happiness is. Let us do a small meditation to collect our thoughts at this point.

SS: Relax and reflect on these thoughts.

Let us sit back and be comfortable ... I look at myself ... I, the creator of every thought and feeling ... There are pressures in life... targets to achieve... deadlines to meet... It's just a pressure ... I am the one who is going to achieve the target ... let me take care of myself as I work towards achieving the target... The quality of my thoughts and feelings as I move towards the target... any fear... any anxiety... any worry... let me first sit back and change the quality of the thought... I am a powerful being... I can achieve what I have decided... but I will first take care of myself... Nothing and no one can influence my state of being... It's totally in my control... I, the powerful being... protected and secure... now move towards my target. This is my journey, a journey of happiness. Om Shanti!

MANTRAS FOR HAPPINESS UNLIMITED

- Stress is a pain that comes to make us realise that there is something I need to change.

- Stress is our creation of negative thoughts, which has an effect on our efficiency, memory power, decision power and, hence, our performance.

- Stress has an impact on our physical and emotional well-being, and hence, any amount of stress is damaging.

- Targets, pressures, deadlines, exams, etc., are natural, but stress is our choice.

- *Stress = pressure ÷ resilience,* that is, inner strength. My first responsibility in any situation is to first take charge of my state of mind because that is the only thing which is in my control.

I Do Not Want Peace
I Am Peace

SO: I read an article in a newspaper recently, which said 'Peace feels happiness. What comes first, peace or happiness? Can you be at peace if you are not happy? The answer to these questions depends on your idea of happiness, on whether you get happiness from external factors or from within'.

SS: Yes, but this is not the first time that we are reading about this. We read and hear about it often, but what happens at the stage of practical implementation? We read about the subject every day in the newspaper, in the spiritual column, in self-help books. Today the largest-selling books are on the topics of self-help, positive-thinking, self-motivation and self-development, spirituality and the likes. Seminars and workshops too are organised often. Yet, what's on the rise is stress, anger and anxiety—and unlimited unhappiness.

So that's the question mark—even though knowledge is everywhere, and there is realization as well, I am looking for happiness outside. This means we haven't taken knowledge and internalized it. Instead, we are accepting stress as natural. So there is a huge difference between what I know, what I am studying, what I believe, and what I am implementing.

SO: You mean to say we do not believe in what we read.
SS: It's not a part of our belief system yet. Stress is natural—it's a belief system and has developed over a period of time, right from our childhood. As a child, we had our parents saying, 'aren't you tensed, you have an exam tomorrow; how can you be so relaxed?' So it's a belief system that developed and got entrenched while I was growing up, and reinforced by society which said – 'obviously stress is natural with so much competition around you'. So it's a deep-rooted belief system and we have lived with it.

Then I read somewhere that 'happiness is your internal way of living, it's your internal way of being, it's how you choose'. But it doesn't change the belief system; I just read it and carry on with my life as I had been doing all along. I say it doesn't work in practical life, and that's where workshops, spirituality and religion get separated from my practical life. I go to a retreat, attend a management workshop or a spiritual programme, and listen to something that is very pure and powerful. While I am listening to it, I absolutely agree that it is true. Then when I come back, I am still my old self and say those things don't work here. It was okay for those people to say what they did, but they are not in my circumstances. We don't even try, we don't experiment. We think it will happen automatically. Well, it won't. Whatever I have studied and whatever I have understood, I will have to put in a little effort at applying it. Now I have understood that anger is unnatural, that it is a response I create; so when I come to my workplace or spend time with my family, I will have to take care that I do not react the next time someone does something that according to me is not right.

SO: You remind me of my Guru. I used to ask her about the way to attain peace, but did not get a direct answer. I was someone who did not know the meaning of peace. Waiting for the lift, I used to keep pressing the button till it reached me. I was a restless man all the time and I said I wanted peace. Your words remind me of that line she said, 'you ask me every time about peace, but do you do any karmas of peace?' I could not relate to what she was saying. When I went outside I saw that somebody had parked his car in front of mine. I wanted to kick that car. I opened my car door and wanted to honk, and I remembered what she had said inside, about doing karmas of peace.

SS: I want peace but I think it has to come from outside. Similarly, I want happiness, I want love, and so on. Want means that someone, somewhere has to do something so that I will get it. On the other hand, spirituality teaches us that I am peace. I have to be at peace while I am doing everything. I am a blissful being; I am a love-full being.

SO: But if I am, then why do I want?
SS: Because I have forgotten that I am. It's like the keys

44

in your pocket or the spectacles on your head. You may be looking for them everywhere and even get others to join you in that search. 'Come on, everyone, look for my keys. Where are my keys?' You look for it everywhere except where they actually are.

SO: How does one realize or even begin to understand that I am peace? How do you prove this?
SS: By experimenting. Everything is a belief, we experiment with it, and if we get the result, we take it as the truth. 'Keep searching for peace, for thats the purpose of life'. If the purpose of life is to keep searching for peace, then when will we find it?

But now we understand this is our nature. Let me experiment—I am a peaceful being. Now I will use this awareness in every act that I do, with every person I meet. Every interaction I have today, I will only remember that I am the one who is doing it. Think of a doctor. He knows he is a doctor, so if someone meets with an accident while he is there on the road, he will immediately get into the healing job. But if the doctor forgets that he is a doctor, even if there are people dying around him he won't do anything because he has forgotten he is a doctor. So healing won't come into action. But the minute he remembers again that I am a doctor, he will start healing. So it's about remembrance. I am a peaceful being was forgotten. Because it was forgotten, I was looking for peace outside. Now try a new belief system. Try—it's still not the truth, it's only a belief. Just experiment with it. If we get the result, then it is the truth.

SO: How will you experiment?

SS: I go back to work today and find that there is a situation. I just remind myself that I am a peaceful being and then act.

SO: I just keep on at this like a 'mantra'. I am a peaceful being, I am a peaceful being. A peon comes and says something that disturbs me and I shout 'shut up'. Again I am angry. Then I start the mantra again, I am peaceful being.

SS: It's not a mantra, it's a conviction. I am telling myself who I am and then preparing myself. Everything that I do will be out of this consciousness. This is who I am. It's a simple thing. Let us say there is a space here in the mind. I think it is empty and say I want happiness, I want peace and I want love. I go to everyone expecting that they will fill my space. Please do this so that I will be happy. Please talk to me nicely so that I will be peaceful. This is one way of living life; this is one belief system. The other belief system is that my space is full but now I have to go through the whole day taking care that its contents don't spill out. That's all—it's full but I have to take care of it. This is the journey; this is what Awakening with Brahma Kumaris is all about. It is about understanding that this is who I am, that now I am peaceful. I just have to remember that while I am talking to you its contents should not spill out.

SO: I am peaceful. The moment I am not peaceful, it spills out?

SS: One way is: I do this so that I will be happy. The other way is: I am happy and now I will do this.

SO: I am happy and I will try to make you happy too.
SS: I don't know whether I will be able to make other people happy because that is another deep-rooted belief system.

SO: What I mean is, when you are around a happy person, you also feel happy because the atmosphere is happy.
SS: True, but someone can be around a happy person and still be very sad unless they take charge of their thoughts and feelings. This is again a deep-rooted belief system that we can make others happy; no one can make the other happy unless they want to be happy themselves.

SO: Then no one can make you sad too.
SS: Absolutely, and that is what it means when I say that I am not dependent on other people for my emotions and my feelings. The most established belief system is—Happiness is dependent on other people.

SO: What does love do to people? She makes me happy, he makes me happy.
SS: When I am with this person, I have nice thoughts and that's why I tell myself I am happy when I am with this person. Then I tell myself that this person makes me happy. This is how we also depend on objects—whether a car or a piece of jewellery—to create similar kinds of thoughts. We use these as stimulus to create a particular kind of thought.

Between the stimulus and the response is my freedom to choose my response. I have the freedom to decide how I am going to respond. Today you talk to me nicely and I am very happy; tomorrow you do something that according to

47

me is not right, and I am hurt. But you are still the same.

SO: I am not still the same; I was different yesterday. I was speaking to you nicely. I am the same person but my behaviour is changed, so you will be shocked by this changed behaviour.

SS: So my response is dependent on your behaviour. Are you always going to behave the way I want you to?

SO: No, I am going to be in different moods on different days, at different times.

SS: Are you wrong?

SO: It is normal.

SS: Are you wrong?

SO: I am right.

SS: According to?

SO: Myself.

SS: But according to me, you are wrong. So I have conditioned myself to believe that this is right and this is wrong. I want people to be right so that I will be happy.

SO: You mean to say you are going to try to control my behaviour, so that you see me as always being nice to you. I should behave as you want me to?

SS: Because then I will be happy.

SO: So are you controlling me?

SS: Yes, I am controlling you, and that's what we are doing everyday with people. We are doing that with our little children, with everyone around us. We want them to be or do or perform or behave in a particular manner because that will make us happy.

Which I think is right, which I think is the way to be. I feel what I think is right and what the other person is doing is wrong, and then my happiness becomes dependent on that.

SO: Then what is a relationship for? Don't you depend on a friend? If I have some problem, I may want you to help me.
SS: That's fine. But my state of mind experiences pain or happiness being dependent on the other person's behaviour.. Let's say I expected you to call me up last evening – if you don't call me, I am hurt. Why? Since my happiness is dependent on your behaviour.

SO: Honestly, I still feel that is natural. If my wife speaks to everybody and not to me, then I will feel hurt.
SS: You still have a choice.

SO: This is what I want to learn.
SS: You have a choice. Okay, she did not call me up, though I thought she should have. I could still be stable by creating different thoughts. I could create the thought that she was busy, or that she did not feel like talking to me at that time.

SO: I think I have got the answer. One of my friends was telling me this incident. He had just reached his house and

saw that it was locked. He had come from an enlightening seminar where there were discussions about various aspects of life. When he saw the locked house, in his usual mood he would have just broken the lock in anger. Instead, he went to his daughter's house, which was just next door, picked up the spare key and opened the door. Just as he went inside, his wife returned. He wanted to confront her first about the locked house, but instead asked her where she had been. She said she had been to the market and had tried to contact him, but his phone was switched off. He realized that he had switched off the phone while the seminar was going on. This meant that she was right and so was he.

SS: Absolutely. Everyone is always right. It's not important whether they are right or they are wrong. First of all I have to be right—not do right but BE right. This means I first take care of myself and this will only happen when I gradually bring myself out of this mental conditioning that my state of mind is dependent on other people. How many people have we held responsible for our pain? Every time we hold other people responsible, we are telling ourselves it's their fault, and I am fine the way I am. But I have to understand that people are doing what they are doing; they could be cheating on me but the pain is my creation. Let's say you are my business partner and you have cheated on me, but the hurt, the resentment and the hatred that I feel are my creation. You cheated me financially and ethically, and that's where your power ends. That's where the power of anybody outside ends, whether it's a business partner, a spouse, or a child.

Our thoughts, feelings and responses are OUR choice.

SO: But something keeps troubling me inside… Why can't I get back at him for what he has done?

SS: Let's say your business partner cheated on you and you parted ways. But now you want to do the same business that he is doing, with the thought, 'I want to come into the market as his competitor and I want to take my revenge. I believe I am right'. So you parted ways since your partner did not conduct himself in an ethical manner. But you want to now start a business with the feeling of taking revenge—is this the kind of energy that you want to bring into your new work? Is this your thought process while starting the new venture? This you have to ask yourself. How you are going to think and feel is your choice. You are hurt and for how long you will remain hurt is also your choice. You want to live with your pain for 10 minutes, 10 days, or 10 years, is your choice. You can sit back, think of the situation, and relive the pain again and again, even years after it happened. Who is the creator of these emotions? It's you. In the same situation, different people will create different responses. So this has to be experimented with at every step.

SO: So if my wife didn't call me when I expected her to, maybe she was busy or my phone was off, but the mind goes on thinking about it. What is that?

SS: Whose mind is it?

SO: My mind.

SS: Who is creating the thoughts?

SO: The mind, not me.

SS: Whose mind is it?

SO: My mind.
SS: So who is creating the thoughts?

SO: I will say my mind is creating the thoughts.
SS: But it's my mind, so who is creating the thoughts? I am. Look at yourself creating those thoughts. She should have called me; I was waiting for her call. So you sit back and just change your thoughts gradually. She didn't feel like talking to me at that time. It was her choice.

SO: She should be happy when she speaks to me, that's what my mind says.
SS: Yes, because I like people to be dependent on me. I am dependent too. It's this control that gives me power. I am empty inside and I love this idea of people being dependent on me. I think I am more powerful because people are dependent on me for feeling good. Because I am dependent on other people, I feel other people should also be dependent on me for feeling happy; how could she be happy without talking to me because I am not happy without talking to her? We are trapped, and we are trapping other people into being dependent on us. And all this is happening in the name of love and respect and trust, which is supposed to be unconditional.

SO: Thank you, Sister Shivani, you have spoken the right words: love, trust, unconditional love. Let us have a minute of meditation.
SS: Relax and Reflect on these thoughts.

Relax and reflect on these thoughts. Meditate.

Let me look at the people around me ... my friends, my family, and my immediate relationships... Everyone around me at home and at work ... doing and being exactly the way they think is right... Their behaviour and their words are the stimulus that's coming from outside... I, the being, choose my response... My response is not automated ... it's not in their control ... it's my choice... Let me look at myself with them ... they are behaving in a manner that I think is not right... Now let me look at myself ... in control ... in charge... not of them ... not of the situation ... but of my state of mind... I am creating the right thought at the right time... I am the master ... an independent ... powerful being. Om Shanti!

MANTRAS FOR HAPPINESS UNLIMITED

- Our belief systems decide our way of living; we need to experiment with what we are learning in order to change our old belief systems.

- I don't want peace. I am peace. Now I will be at peace and do things outside.

- Try a new belief system. Experiment with it. When you experience the result, it becomes the truth.

- Every act I do, I will do it with the awareness that I am a peaceful being.

- Unlimited Happiness is not dependent on people, objects or situations; no one can make me happy and I can't make others happy, till they want it themselves.

- No one is responsible for my hurt, pain, fear, or anger. It is my own creation in response to their behaviour, and I have another choice. The choice to be happy.

BOOK 2

'CHOOSING AWARENESS'

I Have To Be Happy First

SO: Sister Shivani, having told myself that I am the person in charge of my emotions; I cannot play the blame game anymore. But I think it is very difficult to understand what you are saying about not reacting to whatever anybody says. Is this possible?

SS: I do respond, but there is a difference. I am not saying that we do not respond; it's like you are saying something to me and I am just a stone wall with no thoughts, feelings and emotions. That's not right. The question is which thoughts, which feelings, which emotions? It's not that I either react or don't respond at all; reaction means an automated response. Sometimes I have to regret my reactions. How many times we have to say sorry to people?

SO: I end up regretting so many times.
SS: What do we regret?

SO: Unnecessary retaliations.

SS: So we regret our own reactions. You behave in a certain manner and I react, and then I have to come back and apologize.

SO: Because I overreacted as compared to how the other person behaved with me.

SS: It's not about the magnitude of reacting; it's about my not being comfortable with the way I reacted. Normally what happens is that we measure, like you said 'overreacted'. This means we are always measuring our reactions with reference to the other person's behaviour. If you shout at me, I double shout; why? We are always doing it with reference to other people. My personality should be mine, my responses should be mine, and my way of talking should be mine, irrespective of the other person. If I keep changing with reference to everyone I meet, then there will be nothing left in me that is of my own.

SO: Somebody doesn't want to say hello to you, he passes by. You think 'okay, he didn't say hello to me, so why should I?'

SS: Let's say courtesy is your quality; being nice and friendly comes naturally to you; it's your personality. So there you are, walking along a corridor, and you are about to say a very nice, warm 'good morning' to me. However, I just look through and move away. I am cold at this particular moment, due to whatever reason—it may be my nature, my state of mind because of something that had happened. Maybe I am not courteous, and because of me you give up your quality as well. Next, you meet someone else who behaves differently and then you give up another quality. You meet someone who shouts at you and you give up your quality of sweetness. We absorb their negativity and give up our quality.

SO: How does one stick to one's quality?
SS: Just by remembering that this is my personality and this personality is going to be out there during the whole day, interacting with people, irrespective of what is coming from outside. So if we take even one quality, let's say being courteous, it's a simple thing.

SO: Okay, this is my mantra for today: I will be courteous no matter how, where, why, when.
SS: How difficult is that? See, that's what I have to ask myself. My nature is my nature irrespective of how, where, when, what.

SO: We can keep a fast even on the day we have to go to a restaurant or a party. In the same way, you can be strong enough to be courteous today.
SS: Absolutely. Let's take only one quality today. Let's say being courteous is your quality, being humble is your quality, talking sweetly is your quality. Don't let it change.

SO: I have seen the difference in people's behaviour when they are with different people. In fact, there are people who are not as sweet when they speak to their wives, compared to when they speak to another person or an outsider or even somebody else's wife. Why this kind of a change?
SS: We keep changing our personality so many times during

the day that we are not even aware of what our true nature is. To our spouse, we say 'bring the glass of water', and to someone else I say 'can I have a glass of water, please?' Which one of these two is my original nature? It's just that when we are with our spouse, we do not have the responsibility of pleasing them; we take them for granted.

SO: Which one is artificial then?
SS: I have to ask myself.

SO: You mean she will feel nice if I speak in the same way to her?
SS: More important is that you will feel nice if you speak that way to her. Our behaviour is not for other people; it is first for us. Will I speak sweetly to you so that you are happy? No, I will speak sweetly because it makes me feel nice.

SO: Since childhood I have been watching my sisters, brothers, relations, everybody doing something or the other only for the outside world.
SS: That is good. But let's add just one criterion here: taking care of myself first and doing for others what I feel comfortable doing. There are a lot of people who are doing things for others and when they do not get something back in return, they sit back and say, I did so much and what did I get in return—nothing. So, should I be doing it because I want something in return?

SO: Suppose you get only criticism in return. How will you feel?

SS: First of all, I need to check how I was feeling while doing it. Nice. That's about it! Now if I get criticism, I just check whether the criticism is true.

SO: Yesterday I got an email from my niece, saying, 'uncle, you do so many good things for us. But you made me feel very unhappy when you were rude to me.' She recounted two incidents and my first justification was 'it was because I was tired'. Honestly speaking, though, she is right. Yes, I was rude.

SS: Fine, you can apologize now. But that will only happen because you have started looking at yourself. If we give justifications for our rudeness, then there is a whole list of justifications. We like to justify our inadequacies and hide our weaknesses.

SO: Here also I blame my mind. I say my mind plays games with me, I am not doing anything.

SS: My mind, it's mine. It's my responsibility; I am the creator. We speak about our mind as if it was something different from us. We are not ready to take responsibility of our mind, saying it is not in my control. It's like a parent who has given up on their child. Someone comes and says 'your child is not behaving properly', and you reply 'sorry, my child is not in my control, please take care of my child'. But because my mind is not in my control, I try to control your mind. If you say something to me right now and I am not able to control my mind, then I try to control you. I say, 'is this the way to speak', because I am not able to tell my mind 'is this is the way to think'. So I focus on teaching you how to speak, because if you speak nicely then my mind is comfortable.

Let's try one thing. Let's see – how we want to think and feel and be in every relationship.

SO: How I want to think, feel and be in every relationship!
SS: Let's not concentrate too much on what they will think and feel about it. Our attention is always about making other people happy.

SO: That is tiring.
SS: But don't you think we are doing it every day? I want you to be happy, I want my husband to be happy, I want my children to be happy, I want my colleagues to be happy, I want my parents to be happy. So I am doing this, I am speaking like this. It's a very genuine effort, intention is—I want people to be happy with me, because when they are happy, then I will be happy.

SO: It's either this or I say 'forget it, I have no interest in anyone's happiness. It doesn't concern me if someone is happy or not.' How do I keep a balance?
SS: In India, when a girl gets married and comes to her husband's home, sometimes the husband's family expects her to quit her job and be at home. I have met a lot of women who quit their jobs and gave up their careers. Why? 'Because my husband and his family felt that I should not be working. To make them happy I gave up my career; it's been 20 years. But even after 20 years, they are still not happy'. So it's a question mark for the girl. She sacrificed so much, gave up everything that she had studied; sat at home

62

for 20 years for them; and the family is still not happy with her. The woman gets frustrated. As a newly married young girl, when she came into the family it was projected that the family would be happy when she quit her job. To make them happy she quit her job, but in the inside she was not happy about the decision.

SO: They thought that if their daughter-in-law doesn't work, they will be happy. Maybe they are unhappy because of some other reason.
SS: They are not unhappy because of another reason. She has done this to make them happy, but she has been unhappy since the day she gave it all up. She is staying in the same house for 20 years; she chose not to work, but chose it for their happiness. It's not a choice that she made for herself. She has done what they wanted, but she is not happy doing it, so what's the energy that she has been sending to them for the last 20 years? 'I am unhappy, I am unhappy because of you all'. So, how can they be happy?

SO: You mean how can they be happy when she is sending them constant negative energy?
SS: And this is where the secret lies. I cannot make other people happy by doing anything for them. If I choose to do something for them, I have to be sure that I am happy first while doing it—otherwise, I shouldn't do it.

SO: But aren't there certain things to be done whether you are happy or not happy, because they are part of our duties?
SS: You will do the act but you will not give the right energy.

It's like I give you a gift, it's my duty to give you the gift, but when I give it to you, I am upset and uninterested. You won't be happy, you won't even look at the gift because what you are going to get is the energy of the giver. So I did this for you but what was the energy that I was creating while I was doing it? Relationships are not actions; relationships are the energies that we exchange while doing those actions. So if it's my duty, I first convince my mind why I am doing it and then I tell the mind that, 'I am choosing to do this. I am doing this because these people matter to me.' Create the right thought and the right energy first before you do something, otherwise it is best to leave it.

SO: What is the meaning of duty?
SS: Responsibility. We are living with people, and they have certain expectations of how they want me to be and what they want me to do. I consider it my responsibility and my pure desire to make them happy, so I do what they want me to do. But if I do it unhappily, it will not get me the desired results. Moreover, because I am doing it for them, very soon I will be expecting them to do something for me.

SO: It's very difficult for me to understand this.
SS: That's because our focus is all on the doing. Look at the priorities through the day; I have to DO this, I have to DO that. The focus has rarely been - I have to BE like this.

SO: Let's say for homework, children say—I have to do so much work. Isn't that correct?
SS: Yes, they have to do it, but care has to be on how they

are feeling while doing it. They need to be calm, peaceful, happy, and then do it. Let's say I have to run from here to there; I have to be healthy to do it. If I am not healthy and I try to run, the journey will be tiresome, painful and a struggle. Now for everything that I am doing the whole day, my whole life, if I am emotionally healthy, then whatever I do will be beautiful.

SO: So how should we be emotionally healthy?
SS: That's an important aspect. It's important to understand that this is an aspect of my life which we have taken for granted; which we thought will happen on its own; which we thought other people will take care of. We always thought—I am supposed to make you happy and you are supposed to make me happy.

SO: So often I have heard people saying 'when I get married I will be very happy, I am tired of my mother, brothers and sisters'. As it turns out, they are not happy when they get married also and it's back to square one. That's why I asked you this question: how and what to do to be emotionally balanced and stable and to be happy in almost all conditions?
SS: There are people who are not happy in their marriages and looking for relationships outside their marriage.

SO: Then they break that as well and go to the third one.
SS: Because we thought happiness has to come from the other person. So we kept searching.

SO: So finally we come to the conclusion that happiness cannot come from outside at all. We have been working so hard in the wrong direction. We went to temples, we did social work, went shopping, watched movies, parties, alcohol, each time we only wanted to be happy. Now we have to work the other way round.

SS: See, whenever I take the mind to something else, what happens? I am watching a television show or a movie. What happens? Whatever was going on in my mind has been put off for some time. Suppose you have a toothache and you start watching a movie, very soon you will forget the toothache. When you switch off the TV, the pain seems to start again. What happened? Does it mean that the tooth was healed and now it's again hurt? No, it was always in pain but the mind was distracted. My tooth is paining and I am aware of the pain. Who is aware of the pain? The mind is. Then I take my mind to something else, whether it's a conversation, a shopping trip, or a television programme. I feel the pain is gone but it is not—it's just that I am not aware of the pain. Then, when the TV is switched off, I can feel the pain again. Now this is the case of a physical pain, same is when there is an emotional pain. The whole day was tough, I created a lot of stress and anxiety; then I say 'let's go for a movie', 'let's go for a holiday', 'let's take a break from here and go away for 15 days'.

SO: Is it escapism?
SS: It's just that we are trying to take the mind away from there.

SO: Shall we call it temporary happiness?

SS: Not happiness, it's a temporary deviation of the mind from the truth. It's not happiness because we are coming back to it after sometime. See, we can call it happiness if it was healed; your tooth was not healed, it was just that you were not aware of the pain.

SO: So why do we go for holidays, picnics, movies and all that?

SS: It's a change; it's entertainment; it's different from the routine.

SO: Sister Shivani, please tell our readers a little about meditation so that there is 24 x 7 happiness and one is not always dependent on others for it.

SS: Let's just be aware of our thoughts and let's not try and deviate our mind to something else in the pursuit of happiness. We are suppressing the conscious mind by getting distracted and then thinking that this will bring us happiness. The minute the distraction is removed, my conscious mind is back there and it is back with probably more pain. So I need to take charge; this is not the solution, this is just running away from the problem. But for how long can we run away? How long can we be on a holiday? Finally, I am going to be back at work.

Relax and Reflect on these thoughts. Meditate.
Let's look at ourselves ... tomorrow at work ... whatever the situation may be... I am not blaming anyone... I am not going to hold anyone responsible for how I feel ... because I understand

that I am the creator ... just when my mind is about to say it's because of them ... let me just stop and look at myself ... do I have a choice to respond in another way ... what's my nature, my personality ... let it not get influenced by the behaviours and personalities of others... I am the radiator of my qualities irrespective of whatever happens around me... This is self-responsibility... Om Shanti!

MANTRAS FOR HAPPINESS UNLIMITED

- My responses to people should be based on my personality, not on the behaviour of others.

- The way we think and behave, is not for other people. It is first for ourselves because we are the first ones to experience it.

- Let us take charge of our mind, instead of trying to control others and thinking that if they change then my mind will be in control.

- Let us choose how we want to think, feel and be in every relationship. We have always tried to make others happy because we thought when they would be happy, I will be happy too.

- When we do something for others, let us first understand that we chose to do it because they matter to us and we are doing it for ourselves. Only then will we be happy.

- Taking our mind off from problems by watching television, going shopping and other distractions is only a temporary deviation from the pain; it is not happiness because the healing has not happened.

Just One Thought Away

SO: I read somewhere that peace and happiness almost go hand-in-hand. The writer says there is peace in the smile of a child, in the tender touch of one's mother; it has got nothing to do with God or religion but everything to do with the state of one's mind.

SS: Absolutely. In both the instances, the author is talking about the vibrations of the being. The smile of the child emanates vibrations of purity and innocence, and the touch of the mother has vibrations of love and unconditional acceptance. When we experience these gestures, more than the act, it is the vibration in the energy that we experience and that's why there is peace. And wherever there is peace, there will be happiness.

SO: So the mother and the child are so natural. For elders you have to make an effort.

SS: That's what it's all about; about making it natural. The effort happens when you are trying to do it for the other person, while the natural is when you are just being yourself. If I am trying to do things according to what I think will make you happy, then it is an effort; but if I am just being myself, then it's natural.

SO: You mean to say being myself or being natural is peace, love and happiness.

SS: Yes. I just have to be in that awareness that these are my natural qualities. These are not qualities that I will acquire when I do something; it's my natural personality, my natural sanskar. It's my original state of being; I just have to remember it and let it flow—not look for it outside.

SO: All my life I have been hearing people say 'look, I am a December-born', 'I am a January–born', 'I am a Leo', 'I am a Taurus', 'I am a so-and-so'. I am a short-tempered person, my husband is so-and-so, my wife is sweet. It's so easy to attribute things to one's birth and say 'I am like this'. Now we have got to learn that all of this is wrong.

SS: There's a very beautiful word in Hindi – sanskars. It's the personality trait. Every being carries five types of sanskars and that's why it's important to understand the being, because it is a package made up of these five types of sanskars. The first set of sanskars we get from the family. We are within the vibration of the family members, so that energy is automatically influencing us. The second set of sanskars comes from my environment, my country, my religion, caste, city, school and friends. We have always heard—you will be coloured by the company you keep. The environment and the people around you, the energy around you, the belief systems around you, these create sanskars.

The third type of sanskar is sanskars of the past. When I understand that I am a spiritual being and so I don't die —I just change costumes and my journey is through each and every costume. Then there are certain sets of sanskars which I have created in my past costumes. Today I am in this costume, I am doing a lot of actions, it's creating an impression, it's creating a sanskar. It's time to leave this body but the sanskars don't get erased; it's like a recording of songs on the CD which was created and you take that CD and put it on another player, you are still carrying those songs.

SO: Let's forget about past life since we don't know how many of us believe in it.
SS: It's not about believing in it; it's because we don't understand it that we have a lot of conflicts today. You know, the biggest conflict today in a family is that parents expect all their children to be the same, 'Oh, I have given the same upbringing to both my children, then why are they so different'. The parents are same, the family is same, the environment is same, so they naturally expect the sanskars of all the children to be the same. Yet, two children can be twins, born under the same zodiac sign, on the same date and at the same place, and they may go to the same school, grow up in the same environment, but their personalities will be different. Because few years back when they were in two different costumes, they were not in the same family,

they were not in the same country, and they were not in the same environment. They have had a different past, and they are carrying their pasts. We cannot ignore the fact of the past life's sanskars because they are a dominant factor in determining the present. We are not able to understand people because we are only seeing them in their present costume; we are unable to see that they are carrying a past.

SO: It's a nice way for parents to understand their child.
SS: We keep saying, 'look at your brother, you should be like him'. We don't understand that they are two different personalities like the two CDs with two different recordings, which have come to our house, and we are trying to make one similar to the other.

SO: I have heard mothers telling their children, 'look at the other boy and look at you; I often doubt that you are my child; you may have been replaced in the hospital'. How hurting these words must be.
SS: She fails to understand from where her child has got the sanskars that she hasn't given to the child. It's tough for the child too, because even he doesn't know why he has these sanskars. For example, a child could have a sanskar of stealing. He comes from a wealthy family and has everything at home, yet when he goes to school he will pick up another child's pencil. It's something that comes instinctively to him; he doesn't do it logically. That's because the being, the spiritual energy, the soul has carried some sanskars. When we are unaware, the sanskars will come into play automatically.

SO: Sister Shivani, it's difficult to reach this level of awareness. Often there is such a small gap between a thing happening and my reaction. In that split second how will I remember that I should not react like this? I used to see, many Guru, there would be a huge explosion during Diwali and his eye would not even blink. How do we reach that stage?

SS: It comes with attention and practice. Earlier if I was conducting a workshop and somebody's mobile phone rang, I would get disturbed. There I was talking to the gathering about stability, but inside I was disturbed.

SO: So it was one step leading to another? Earlier you were disturbed, another time you must have said, 'it's okay, they are like that'. Next time, you are not even bothered if they are 'like that' or not; it really doesn't matter to you. It doesn't distract you anymore. Aren't these the stages then? One has to go through stages; one cannot go straight to your stage.

SS: Some people will say 'it's going to take years and years'. No, it doesn't take years, it's just one thought of awareness—otherwise I can get irritated by a mobile phone for a lifetime. We can live our lives getting irritated by the mobiles that are ringing around us.

SO: What is the meaning of one thought of awareness?

SS: One thought is—'How can I allow one unimportant ringtone to disturb my mind?' This is just one thought.

I don't think about the opposite person because it is

not the ringtone that disturbs us; it's the thoughts that I create after listening to the ringtone. Why did they not switch off their mobiles? Don't they know that they are in a public programme? It's courtesy that you switch off your mobile. So it's not the ringtone that irritates me; it's the thoughts that I create in response to the ringtone that irritate me. The ringtone is just a trigger. I have to realize what is disturbing me. It is my own thoughts. My thought is that they should be polite enough to switch off the phone. Now I change my thought: it's their choice, whether they want to switch it off or not, and I respect their choice.

SO: I used to get disturbed even if somebody walked in front of me while I was acting my scene. Now I can see so many people moving around, and now I am learning to accept it'.

SS: Now this is where we are creating the fourth type of sanskar. Getting irritated was one of the past sanskars, whether it came from the past birth, or from the current environment. With awareness we can change our sanskar. This is creating sanskars with our own will power. So we cannot keep blaming—oh, I can't help it, this must be a past sanskar. It's all about awareness.

SO: You are saying that awareness will bring will power.

SS: Yes. It's will power that I will use to create a new sanskar. See, every time I say 'this is because of you'; 'I am getting irritated because of this'; I imply that I am not powerful and others can overpower me. Will power means I have the power to choose, to think and be and do what I want. Every time I use that power, it's will power. Many times we feel we don't have will power. Everyone has power, everyone has the same amount of will power; it just depends on how much we are going to use it. It depends on how we are going to sit back and stop blaming others. We disempower ourselves by not using our will power.

SO: I met someone who took two days to quit his habit of drinking of 30 years. You mean to say I have the same amount of will power as him? If yes, then what is it that I am unable to see that I have will power or what is it that's stopping me from using it?
SS: It's simple: I am not using it. A human quality is useful only if it is being used.

SO: But what if I don't know whether I have a quality or not? I don't know how to see or use the quality.
SS: That's why we are learning. It's that area of life on which we now start focusing attention. If we say we don't have time for spirituality; we don't have time to meditate; then we are choosing not to use the powers that we have. We are choosing not to apply the tools that are there.

It's like I have a whole lot of property in my locker but I am refuse to open it and use it for myself and helping others; rather, I go around begging people for love, peace and happiness because I don't want to use the time to go into my own locker, open it and use it from there.

SO: So your locker is meditation?
SS: It's here in the mind and the key is with us, and only we

know how to open it.

SO: So there is no need to go to anyone for getting my locker opened, for developing my powers.
SS: If we go somewhere, somebody out there could be instrumental in telling us how to open it, but finally no one else can open it for us. No one can activate the will power for us; that someone can only help us realize that we have this power. A simple example is when we want to give up our addictions. Someone may want to give up alcohol, or cut down their TV watching time, or Internet surfing. We create a powerful positive thought,

'Today I will watch TV only for an hour.' We are aware of this positive thought we create, but we are not aware of so many negative thoughts we create immediately, 'It is difficult for me ... I love watching TV ... I have tried many times but I always fail

... It's my habit ... Can't go in one day ... Obviously it will take time'. Now we created one positive thought to empower ourselves, and then followed by so many negative thoughts which will disempower us. Once you have decided to do something, just create one single thought and start working on it.

SO: If we all have the same will power, then how is it that some are able to give up their addictions sooner than others.
SS: Everyone has equal will power because everyone is a powerful being; realizing my own will power depends on how much I am aware that I am a powerful being and how

much I use it. Of course, the people around me also make a difference.

You know, we are largely responsible for reducing the will power of those around us, especially our children. Let's say your child spends too much time on the Internet and you tell him that from tomorrow he is going to be on it only for an hour. Your words are affirmative, but your thoughts are of doubt and failure in giving up the addiction.

SO: Internally I am so sure that my child will not be able to do it.
SS: Every thought that I create is the energy that I am showing or radiating to the child.

SO: But why should the child get disturbed by the energy of the parent?
SS: We get influenced by the thoughts, words and actions of other people. We have to be very strong and protected and that can happen if we practice not getting influenced by the energy around us. Right now we are quite vulnerable. So everything that's happening around us creates an impact. We should take care of ourselves and the people around us, if someone is trying to do something, do not create a single thought of doubt or negativity. If we create thoughts of doubt and fear for the child, we disempower the child. Let us create only powerful thoughts, 'you can do it, we have faith in you'. Even if the child does not have the power, he will get empowered by the parents and succeed. Today in the corporate sector they are saying we motivate our people. Motivation will not happen with words. Your subordinate

is late every day; you motivate him by saying 'I am sure you will do it'. But your thinking is 'I know him, he is not going to come on time; he will always be like this'.

Thoughts and words are different. So when we say we are family and we are friends and we are there for each other, let it not be just in words. There should be harmony between thoughts and words, and that's the simplest thing to take care of in relationships. Let there be no conflict between what we are thinking and what we are saying. When there is a difference, there is also a conflict in the energy that the opposite person receives. Remember, that the thought energy travels faster.

SO: Don't you think today's world is like this? We say 'wow, you are wearing such a nice shirt!' Inside we are thinking 'he doesn't have taste'.
SS: Why did we say 'wow, you are wearing a nice shirt'?

SO: A lot of people talk like that. We pick it up from everyone around.
SS: But why do I say to you that your shirt is very nice?

SO: To please people.
SS: To please people. This is extremely important. We are saying it to make people happy. Now, happiness is not words; happiness is energy, it is vibrations, it is feelings. I am sending a word out by paying a compliment to your shirt, and I am also sending other thoughts saying horrible shirt, horrible choice, no taste at all. So what's the total energy that comes to you? In fact vibration reaches faster and is much more

79

powerful than the words.

SO: He will know that I did not like his shirt.
SS: He won't be able to catch your thoughts. We can't catch people's thoughts. The mind needs to be really very silent to be able to catch people's thoughts, but we can catch the feelings, the vibrations. That is why sometimes after meeting people and having a polite conversation, we still feel, 'I don't think they really meant what they said; they were nice to talk to but I don't feel anything nice after they left.' The foundation of this relationship is false, so it's no relationship at all. If I send this conflicting energy to you, you will doubt my intentions and then you will always doubt my intention. Then there is no trust in this relationship; one word and the relationship is over because there was no foundation. So we need to ask ourselves what are we doing.

One option is: I don't say that you are wearing a nice shirt if I am not convinced that it is nice. If I don't feel it's nice, I shouldn't say it's nice; it's integrity. If at all I still want to say it's nice, first let "me" understand that it's nice, by creating a thought: okay I might not like a white shirt but that's just my choice; your choice is nice for you. Create this thought and then say it. I keep working on myself till my thought and words are in harmony and then I communicate. That is communication.

SO: If I say you are wearing something nice and actually I do not mean it, what happens to me? What am I doing to myself, to my soul, to my personality?
SS: I am cheating myself. I am not honest to myself; what I

think, I don't do. There is disharmony between my thoughts, words and actions; I think something else, I say something else; and I do something else. There is disharmony and this disharmony will then continue. Again I will think I have to do this, but my words and actions will not follow, which will reduce my will power. It's going to be damaging for us and that is why our will power is low today.

SO: We understood the four types of sanskars, which is the fifth type?
SS: The fifth sanskar are the original sanskars. When I understand my original sanskar, it is easy to take care of the other four. Past birth sanskars—not in my control; sanskars from family—not in my control; sanskars from the environment—not in my control; will power—in my control. I can create new sanskars through my will power but even will power gets activated when I understand my original sanskar, my original nature, and that's the original nature of every human soul on this planet. Every being is originally pure, affectionate, peaceful, blissful and powerful. Every being has this nature and we are looking for it outside because we have forgotten that this is my nature. Spirituality shifts our belief from I want happiness and peace to the truth that I am a peaceful being; I am a blissful being; I am a powerful being.

And then it becomes natural and the whole perspective will change. If I want peace, then I am always seeking outside. If I understand, I am peace, then I become a giver. So it ends our looking for happiness, asking for love, and we start sharing our peace, love and happiness with all. It automatically flows from us to the people around us. Like when we are stressed, we don't have to consciously give it to others, all who come in our energy field automatically receive it and get influenced by us. Similarly by being in our natural state of peace and happiness, we don't have to give it, it will naturally radiate and will be felt by family and friends. Energy is like an infection—we catch it from the people around us.

SO: Thank you, Sister Shivani. You have told us something beautiful: I am peace. I am love. I am knowledge. I am bliss.

MANTRAS FOR HAPPINESS UNLIMITED

- Our personality is a combination of five types of sanskars - personality traits.

- Some sanskars we get from our parents and other family members. We call these hereditary sanskars because we are within the influence of their vibrations.

- There are sanskars we create because of our environment: our nationality, religion, culture and friends.

- A very important set of sanskars are those that we carry from our past birth. Our soul carries its personality traits created in one costume to the next costume.

- We create the fourth type of sanskars through our own will power. Everyone has the same amount of will power; it just depends on realizing that we have will power and then using it favourably.

- The fifth set of sanskars are the original sanskars of every soul, these being purity, peace, love, bliss, knowledge, power and truth.

I Am Aware. I Am Creating

SO: Sister Shivani, I have been thinking about the hide-and-seek that the mind plays. The moment I try to see where it is, it vanishes; when I go to my thoughts in order to be aware of them, the thoughts stop, and the moment I am somewhere else, they come back to me. Where is this mind and what is it? How may one control it in day-to-day life? Is it through meditation?

SS: Let me share this story with you that I read a few days back, about a disciple who goes to his guru and asks for one word so that he can achieve what his guru has achieved. The guru says 'awareness'. The disciple writes down the word on a piece of paper and leaves, thinking he will do this now. When he reaches halfway, he wonders 'but what am I supposed to do?' So he goes back and asks his guru, 'what does the word mean?' Guru says 'awareness means awareness'. The disciple says okay and leaves again. But, after sometime he comes back and asks, 'but what does it mean and what am I supposed to do?' The guru says, 'awareness means awareness means awareness', which means do not try and to find a logic behind it. Awareness means just be aware of your thoughts; just watch your thoughts. We are aware of everything that is happening in the world. We are aware of what is happening under the ocean; we are aware of what is happening on the moon; we are aware of what is happening on other planets; we are aware of what is happening in the neighbour's house; we are aware of what is happening everywhere. So, awareness means to know what's happening. Now, awareness means just to know what's happening...

SO: Within me?
SS: Nothing within. That again is very complicated. When you say look within, it's very complicated. Look within, but where? Look at what? What are we supposed to do? Look within means just look at the thoughts that I create. Take a walk early in the morning; it's not about just looking at who is walking, who is wearing what, who is listening to music, who is talking about what, what has happened in the newspaper; just talk to yourself. What am I thinking? You can practise this the whole day.

SO: People will say this guy is talking to himself and has gone mad.
SS: You won't come to know when I am talking to myself. Just stop and check—What am I thinking?

SO: But the moment I stop to check what I am thinking, that thought stops. Some other thought then takes over

me away for the next few hours, before I come back to what I was thinking.

SS: This is because I haven't done it in a very long time. Once I do it regularly, I won't need to stop and look at what I am thinking. I will always be aware of what I am thinking. Suppose today has not been a nice day at work; so I come back and I am sitting with the paper. The television is on but my mind is working—it's not interested in the running television. I am thinking—this shouldn't have happened, this is not the way things should have happened today, this is not the way they should have spoken to me. I have been working so hard, but I just don't get recognized for my work. Who is thinking all this? I am thinking. That's all; this is awareness; this is what I am thinking. The Second stage of awareness is: is this the right kind of thinking for me? And Third stage of awareness is: can I change it? That's all.

SO: What will happen if I am not thinking? I have to think something.

SS: Yes, there is never a stage when we are not thinking.

SO: Either some kind of song goes on, or some kind of a jingle, or something said by somebody... it goes on and on; the mind is all the time on. And you mean to say one has to switch it over to something else, to feed it something else.

SS: It's like water, flowing constantly. I can't stop it but I can always channelize it; I don't have to flow this side, I can flow the other side. So I just change the direction of the water, give it a new direction to flow. Similarly, I don't stop thinking. A lot of people think meditation means to stop thinking, and so they will concentrate on a point of light and say 'no thoughts – no thoughts – no thoughts'. 'I don't have to think' is also a thought.

It can never happen. The mind can never stop thinking. We are trying to do something that is not natural. That's why I say I am feeling very heavy here. There is too much of pressure here because I have tried to suppress something. It's not natural.

SO: So much pressure to stop thinking that you are going to get up tired and disappointed.
SS: Exactly. I have not been able to achieve it and then I say I tried meditation but couldn't do it. It happens with many people. There is so much going on in the mind, it is like a car that is in the fifth gear and I suddenly want to bring it down to neutral. I am trying to do it in one go. What's going to happen? I get a jerk.

SO: Sister, shall we go back a little? You said be aware—okay, I start being aware. Then what happens? I just honestly want to know what happens practically.
SS: Practically, the first thing that happens is knowledge.

SO: You said be aware—okay, I start being aware. Then what happens? Now I am aware that I am speaking to you. This is my thought and my question. So now that I am aware of my thought, what next?
SS: First thing is to be aware that I am creating this thought. A very common illusion is that the thought is coming to

87

me because of some stimulus. You know, a lot of people use this language: 'that thought just came to me'. What does it mean?

SO: He reminded me of that, he made me think, he made me do. The language is wrong?
SS: Yes! The expression is all wrong because the belief systems are confused inside. 'I was just hit by those feelings, by those thoughts'. As if something comes from outside...Thoughts don't come to us; feelings don't come from outside. However tough the situation may be, I am the creator of the thought. The minute I understand I am the creator of the thought, the blame game is over.

SO: So I am aware of my thought. The next step is to know that I am the creator of this thought. Then I will analyze why waste a thought. It is such a bad thought, it's going to hurt me, disturb me. Let me improve on this. Am I right?
SS: Absolutely. I will be able to change the thought once I have taken the responsibility that I am the creator.

SO: Responsibility is hard work. I may say I am ready to take responsibility but I never really understand it.
SS: Because the focus is so much outside. The attention is always outside. We were aware of what is happening outside. Then we felt things happening inside. But because we were focused on the outside, we were not aware that what was happening inside was our creation and we had a choice.

SO: I remember what you told me once. Suppose a child hits a table and falls. You say this table is to blame and it is a bad thing; let's beat this table. The child feels better when you say this; he doesn't even understand that it's his mistake. So the conditioning of such a thinking begins in childhood. This table is in the wrong place.

SS: This is true. I should be made to understand that the table is where it is supposed to be; it is I who failed to see the table while playing.

Yes, I have to understand this. Let's say my boss shouted at me this morning. I had worked very hard; I was sincere; I finished everything on time. But he still shouted at me. My mind starts, 'He just doesn't respect sincerity; he doesn't know how to appreciate and motivate his people'. These thoughts are coming to me; it is how I feel. And who is responsible for this? It's my boss, and I am justified in thinking like this. Then I say my boss needs to change. And there goes the self-awareness and the inner responsibility.

SO: So if I am aware first, then I will know that I am creating this thought towards my boss and I am also sending out negative energy to him. Then, while sending this energy to him, I am also creating so much negative energy within me. So it is all give-and-take of negative energy and I am surrounded with that.

SS: Not only that, the energy that I am creating and sending to him is also affecting those around me. My family, with whom I am sitting at home in the evening, is feeling that energy too because I am creating it. You know, it's like a perfume. Like it or not, I do get the smell of the perfume that you use. That's why if we are under stress we automatically pass it on to our children.

SO: This reminds me of something quite interesting. When I am stressed and angry and come home in that state of mind, my dog, instead of greeting me, just goes into a corner.

SS: Now we will just change the way we think. In the whole day we are creating about 40 to 50 thousand thoughts. This translates into 25 to 30 thoughts per minute, created without awareness. Every time we say this is coming to me. So one can imagine what quality of life one is living. It's like you are the chairman of a company that has 40,000 to 50,000 products coming out of the factory on a daily basis and you are not aware of the product quality. Hence, there is chaos.

Broadly, we can classify thoughts into four types. Pure, powerful, positive thoughts are one category. They will be absolutely clean and selfless. These attributes are rare today. Selfless means thinking more about the needs and happiness, etc. of other people than about your own, with no expectation attached. Wherever there will be an expectation it will be followed by hurt, so it's not positive anymore. Negative thoughts: Resentment, hatred, criticism, anger, and these come in large numbers. Necessary thoughts: I have to do this, I have to go here, I have to meet so and so. They are neither positive nor negative; they are neutral. But let's be careful that the neutral does not get followed by the negative. Let's say 'I have to go to the airport.' It's a necessary thought. 'I hope there is no traffic jam on the way; I hope I will reach in time.' So, a neutral thought may be followed by negative thoughts. The neutral thought will be one but it is followed sometimes by a series of negative thoughts. The fourth type of thought is waste thoughts, things that are not in my control. Thinking about that which is not in my control is a waste of time and energy—that is I am thinking either about the moment that has passed or about a moment that is still to come. Both are not in my control. The past and the future are not in my control.

SO: Past, future, or thinking about other people, they are a waste.
SS: Even when I am thinking about other people – they should have done this, why did they do this, I want them to do this—it's either in the past or in the future. I don't accept them in the present moment as they are. If we just practise this for one day, if we are just aware about this for one day, we will be shocked. At any moment just check what you are thinking.

You will be thinking either about something that has already happened or about something that is still to happen. So we are living either in the past or in the future. Both are a waste because both are not in my control.

SO: I remember once I was driving home from my shooting and was thinking of my scene that I had just rehearsed. I was driving alone and thinking. I wish I had done that. As the scene kept playing in my mind, I crossed my home. I had to take a U-turn and go back.
SS: Actually we can cross our whole life if we are like this, thinking about the past or the future. Just be constantly aware

that first is knowledge that I am the creator of the thought and second that there are these different types of thoughts. Negative and waste thoughts are damaging. Waste thoughts are a waste of energy and this waste, in turn, is followed by further negative thoughts. The minute I go into the past, the thoughts run along these lines: Oh! It should have been like this; it should not have been like that; Those days were better; they shouldn't have said this. If I go into the future, my thought can be: When this happens then I will be happy. This means now I am not happy. It's not a nice thought.

SO: Now I understand why people say 'I didn't do anything today why am I so tired?' If he had gone to play a game of golf, he wouldn't have been so tired.
SS: Yes then the mind wouldn't have been creating so many negative and waste thoughts, while it was concentrating on something else.

Forty to fifty thousand thoughts in a day! If they are not of the right quality, what will happen to the system inside? A psychiatrist will tell us that, on an average, 80 per cent of the time the mind is in the past and 15 per cent of the time it is in the future and so 95 per cent is gone as waste.

SO: And out of the 80 per cent wonder how much is positive.
SS: There is nothing positive in the past because if it was a pleasant past and I am thinking about it, then I am thinking that those days were better. So there is nothing positive there. People say it is good to have nice memories. Yes, it's a memory, but it's past. It's over. What is important is now.

SO: How often people speak about the past when you meet them. You should have seen the salutes I received when I was in the army, when I was a general; I was this; I was that.

SS: What you are feeling inside right now is this: those were the days when I got all of that from everybody, but today I don't have that kind of attention. So, by saying all this about my past, I am trying to seek attention from people around me.

These are only words. We say very few words compared to how much we think. There could be 25 to 30 thoughts per minute but not 25 to 30 sentences in the same time. One may not be using even 4 to 5 sentences in a minute. Every thought has an effect on the entire system, on every cell of the body. Thoughts are the most powerful source of energy that we have, so let's be careful about how we use them. It's like you possess nuclear energy—you can use it for healing and you can use it to destroy the world. The energy is the same. You have your MRI, CT scan, etc., done with nuclear energy on one hand, and you also have all the nuclear missiles on the other hand. They are the same energy. Every form of energy can be used for constructive as well as destructive purpose. It's the same with thought energy. It can give and create love, peace, purity; it can give and create hatred, resentment, worry, anxiety. It's the same thought energy but the wonderful part is that these are my thoughts, so I have a choice.

SO: I am still thinking about what you said just now about every thought having an effect on my body. If I am going to think thousands and thousands of thoughts in a day and millions of thoughts in a month or my lifetime, what

will happen to my body?

SS: See, mostly for an illness the doctors will tell us it's psychosomatic, that is the connection of the mind and the body. So heal the mind, the body will follow. Of course you must take care of the body, but it will not be of much use if we take care only of the body and don't heal the mind. That's why someone will say I am a strict vegetarian; I don't smoke; I don't drink; I exercise every day, and yet I had a heart attack in my 30s or 40s. That's because I took care only of the body, while the mind was under stress.

Relax and Reflect on these thoughts. Meditate.

Let me just sit back, relax, and really look at my mind now. No one will come to know that I am looking. It's something that goes on inside. And I am going to do it the whole day, while I am working, while I am talking, while I am driving, while I am walking; it's about just being aware of my thoughts.

My thoughts, my creation ... something that I thought was happening automatically ... I now realise the seed is me... I am the creator of every thought ... every thought has an influence on my body ... and on everyone around me... Let me look at my thoughts ... flowing beautifully ... in control ... because I realize I am the master... Whatever happens around me ... pleasant or not so nice ... whatever anyone may do or say ... however anyone may behave... I just sit back and look at my thoughts ... and gradually channelize the thoughts into a different direction ... because I am the master and the creator... I turn the focus from outside to inside ... because I understand now that the energy flows from inside me to everyone outside... So I am doing everything outside but my attention is on what I am

94

creating inside ... because what I create inside naturally flows outside... I am honest with myself ... honest in my thoughts ... words and actions ... and there is absolute harmony. This is trust... I trust myself ... I love myself ... because I am a pure being... Om Shanti!

MANTRAS FOR HAPPINESS UNLIMITED

- Self-awareness means to just watch my thoughts, to be able to see what I am thinking, and to be aware that I am the creator of these thoughts.

- Next step is to check whether this thinking is the right kind of thinking for me.

- We create 25 to 30 thoughts per minute – that is, 40 to 50 thousand thoughts in a day. Thoughts are the most powerful source of energy that we have, so let's be careful about how we use them.

- There are four types of thoughts. One type of thought is pure, powerful, positive and selfless; another type is negative thoughts of ego and anger that create hatred, resentment, fear, rejection, or criticism.

- Next are Necessary thoughts that are thoughts related to action; these are neutral thoughts, they can be precursors to negative thoughts.

- The fourth type of thought is waste thoughts, which are thoughts about the past or the future—both not in our control, and so a waste of time and energy.

Think. Believe.
The Rest Will Follow

SO: Sister Shivani, we have been speaking about awareness, thought and mind, and it was a wonderful meditation that you shared with us. After doing it, I started speaking softly (I usually speak loud) and my hand movements were not jerky. Everything felt peaceful, light and stable.

SS: That goes to prove that if you take care of the mind, everything else is taken care of. It is the mind that has an effect on the body. It is the mind that creates the words and it is the mind that finally comes out into actions. When we are talking about transformation—I want to change this habit; I want to change this part of my personality; I want to change this particular behaviour—we always try to bring about the transformation outside. The way I walk, the way I talk, the way I speak to people, the way I behave... we tell others also to behave like this or that. This transformation is always temporary because the seed is the thought. Not changing the thought it self will have a temporary effect; the change will last for a few days and then we are back to the old self. However, if I change the thought, I won't even be aware but suddenly I will find so much transformation outside.

SO: So we won't need to work on each and every aspect of our body, our movement, our speech, the way we look, the way we talk. It is just like what an actor does in method acting. Method acting teaches us to go from within to the outside. Once I start believing that I am so and so, then I don't have to check on my walk, on the way I speak, it happens naturally once I believe in it.

SS: I am creating the character inside; the whole sketch is there inside. Who does this inner work? The mind does.

SO: When you believe in it, then things follow. You are not acting anymore; you are living, you are playing.

SS: You are naturally flowing. Similarly, I am a peaceful being. I have created the character inside, so now I don't have to take care of how to speak, how to walk, how to behave. Once I am convinced inside that I—the actor—am a peaceful being, then everything that the actor will do will be through the vibration of peace.

SO: So that means I should play the role of a peaceful personality. Suresh Oberoi as a peaceful being, happy being...

SS: You have to come back to the root first. I the peaceful being who has this name, this body and plays this role.

Whether it's an actor, a doctor, a lawyer, it doesn't matter what the role is.

SO: So the peaceful being doesn't have to learn each and every step since he is peaceful.

SS: Each one of us is an actor and playing so many roles. In your lifetime…

In your lifetime, let's say you played three hundred roles but every role had that stamp of you as the actor—only you played it in that way. Even if another actor copies you and plays the same roles, he will be different from you because he has his own style. So the actor's personality will always reflect in every role he plays. So now I have to remember, who am I the actor and what are the roles I play? So whichever role I play—a father, a husband, a friend, a boss—the actor's personality has to show in every role. Now who am I the actor? I am a pure, peaceful, love-full being. And it doesn't matter whether I am talking to a friend or whether I am talking to my son, the peaceful personality will be there in both. The reason I am different with different people is that here I am a friend, and there I am a father.

SO: I have to play a father here, so I will order my child.
SS: So I am more conscious of the role rather than the actor who is playing the role. Old belief systems tell me that a father should be like this. So I am behaving according to some set patterns of how a father should be. A father should always be authoritative, controlling and strict.

SO: If I am different with one person, speak differently to the other person, it means I am behaving in contrast

to my character? There is no consistency?

SS: I am only role-conscious. I am a friend to this person, so I should speak like this. Here I am the boss, so this is the way to behave with my juniors. The actor inside is just not aware.

SO: But Sister Shivani, everybody behaves differently at different places and times. One is different in office, at home, with wife, with friends, and so on.

SS: Which one of these is our original nature?

SO: I don't know which one is original. I am confused. There are so many different roles.

SS: Let's take a simple example. We walk into an office and within 10 minutes we meet four people: one from the security, one at the reception, then someone in middle management, and finally the top chairman. Four people in 10 minutes, and four times our behaviour changes. My way of talking to the security guard and my way of talking to the chairman are different. Out of these four which one is my original personality?

SO: I am confused. I am playing different roles all the time. I don't have a consistent role.

SS: My original personality is not there because I am changing every time. I talked to a security guard, I talked to a receptionist, and accordingly I changed. Next I talked to a manager and so I changed; then I talked to a chairman, and again I changed. I'm connecting to positions, to status, to physical looks, to all the things that are acquired.

SO: But if I ask this question to anybody, they will say what is wrong in doing that. So isn't it normal, since everybody does it?

SS: We don't know if it's normal, but yes, we have been doing it for a very long time. We are talking and connecting to people on the basis of everything that's acquired. Today you are the chairman, tomorrow you are not, so tomorrow my relationship with you will change. In that case, that was not a relationship at all. And that's why relationships are so fragile. I can change the minute anything that you have acquired has changed. We are forgetting who we are. This acquired self is the ego; acquired by knowledge, by position, by wealth, by property. Everything that I have acquired, it's not me, it belongs to me. But when I am in the consciousness of 'this is what I have acquired' and 'this is what you have acquired', it is the acquired who are talking to each other. And that's why there isn't a strong foundation; it's the ego of one talking to the ego of the other. When egos are talking, it is a position talking to a position, a bank balance talking to another bank balance. What about the pure being talking to another pure being?

This is where we really need to stop and realize that we are always connecting only to the outside, while the actor is sleeping inside. Even if I find that the actors around me are sleeping and I wake up, the others will wake up gradually. When you are doing theatre, what do you do when one actor forgets his lines?

SO: I either use his line or give him a cue, or try to help out or improvise it so that the act goes on.

SS: But for you to be able to do that, what do you have to concentrate on first? Suppose I am the actor and I forget my script. For you to help me with my part, you will have to first pay attention to your script, right? You have two options. One, you pay attention to your script and just flow in the right way so that I will get the cue and I will also start flowing in the right direction. Two, you get affected by the fact that I have forgotten my script, because of which your attention deviates from your script and you are more interested in telling me how I should be speaking, what I should be speaking.

Now, in the whole day, check how much are we concentrating on other people's script... *what they should be doing, what they should be saying, how they should be behaving. In the process we are not aware of our own own script, what I should be thinking, what I should be saying.* Throughout the day, how many times are we writing other people's script? We actually sit in front of the television writing the script for the prime minister, for the cricketer, for the film actor; *they shouldn't be acting like this, they shouldn't be wearing this, this is not how they should have done this.* We are just wasting time and energy by trying and writing their script. Let's write only one script – our script, because that is the only one that will be followed. I can keep on writing your script – *how you should be, how you should talk, how you should perform, how you should behave.* Are you going to go according to my script? No. What a waste of time and energy! I am sitting and writing the scripts of so many actors and none of them are going to use my script.

SO: I find it so silly that I am doing something that is of no use and wasting time.

SS: At a time you can write only one script; if I am writing yours, I am definitely not writing mine. Look at it this way. You start saying something to me which I do not like; you start shouting at me. Now, instead of taking care of how I should be, I'm telling you this is not how you should be talking to me. While I am trying to change your script I go out of control, and soon I forget my own script and I am shouting louder than you did. When I start to write your script and forget my own lines, what will happen to the play?

SO: Disaster.

SS: That's what's happening everywhere around. If we just start focusing on our script, everyone else will take their cue. Someone next to you is getting angry, has lost his temper, is going out of control, but if you remain in control he will soon come back into control because you have retained your composure. You are writing your script and they will come back to their original quality of peace. The other possibility is that soon everyone will forget their script and go out of control. This is a choice we need to make—that of writing our own script, because that's the only one that will be followed in any case. The others will go into the category of waste thoughts. So let's be aware of this, because this is awareness. I am aware of how many times in the day I just keep thinking about what other people should be doing and saying.

SO: But why can't I just stop myself and ask what is the point, why am I wasting time?

SS: Now we will do it because we are aware; earlier we were not aware, so we thought it was natural to think like that. It's like you see a tap running and you immediately close it because water is getting wasted.

SO: Our energy depletes, right?
SS: It depletes because we are thinking of something that is not in our control.

SO: This reminds me of something interesting you said, "For each and every thought we have, there is some reaction in the body."
SS: The health of our body reflects the quality of our thoughts.

SO: Many things are clear to me now. Earlier I thought, what is this, how is it possible, how can I not be angry when this happens? It's so natural to be angry. I remember the time when I didn't have money and I could not sleep all night because someone who owed me money cheated on me. It was so painful and I used to beat him up in my thoughts. I ended up with high blood pressure.
SS: In this particular situation, someone has cheated you of money. There's no denying that it's a grave situation and it's natural for you to be upset and angry, but let us keep our loss up till there. I have lost money but this is not in my control; somebody else is responsible for the lost money. But what I lose, is my peace of mind, health of my body, harmony in my relationships, so there I am the reason.

Then I can say that he cheated me; it's because of him I lost the money. But for anything else that I lose, I am the reason, I am the cheater. This is what I do to myself

SO: I am being irresponsible. I thought it was natural.
SS: Just remember one thing: what I think I am doing to others, I am actually doing it to myself. If I am giving a cold shoulder to the other person, talking angrily to the other person, it is actually a cold shoulder to me, it's anger towards me, because whatever I am creating is first getting created in my mind. This means I am the first one who experiences it. The cold shoulder that I give you might not affect you at all, but since I created the thought, I am bound to get affected. So when you are doing something for other people, good or bad, just remember that it's less for them and more for yourself.

SO: A healthy thought, a healthy body, a healthy life.
SS: Nurture my pure thoughts, loving thoughts, forgiving thoughts. Somebody has done something wrong, but I just forgive and forget. I am not forgiving him—I am forgiving myself. If I keep holding on to the resentment and the hatred, it's not for the other person, it's here and it's in me. I am going to be creating it and I am going to be experiencing it. So, the entire responsibility comes back to me.

SO: The other day I met a Brahma Kumar who told me about the time when somebody cheated him of fifty thousand rupees. It was a big amount for him. And you know what his reaction was? He said, 'May God give him so much that he does not repeat this act with anybody else; he must be in need of money; may God give him ten times more so that some other person is not cheated

like I have been'. After about eight years, the man who cheated came back with the money.

SS: Your acquaintance sent him good vibrations, good wishes, pure energy. The person came and returned him the money after eight years; the question is what was the quality of the mind for those eight years? Your acquaintance created this thought that maybe the other person who took the money needed it badly and was needy; he even blessed the person saying that may he have much more;' in other words he was at peace. The other option for him was to harbour hatred, resentment and revenge for eight years. He would still get back the money after eight years, but in those years he would have done so much damage to himself that the money would not be able to repair it.

SO: Here everyone may not agree with you and me. They will say this is a weakness. Why should I keep quiet? I will hit him back. Let's explore this subject further as our conversation progresses. For now, let's do a small meditation.

SS: Relax and Reflect on these thoughts. Meditate.

Let me just look at myself... I, my own friend, honest with myself... Let me look at the various reactions I give to other people during the day... Anger ... jealousy ... criticism ... hatred ... seemed to be normal in return for what they have done to me... But now I need to stop and ask myself ... who am I giving it to... It's a creation that I experience first ... it's an energy that I am feeding to my own mind... Let me stop and ask myself ... who is the one who is hurting me ... who is the one who is creating the pain ... I have a choice ... I the pure and peaceful being ... the actor playing so many different roles with other actors ... each

105

one playing their role... I the actor remember my true personality ... the pure being... I play every act and every role with the awareness of my original personality... Look at yourself ... that pure being as the parent ... the friend ... the boss... Everywhere I go ... it's me ... the pure being. Om Shanti!

MANTRAS FOR HAPPINESS UNLIMITED

- If we change our thoughts, our words and actions too will change. Hence, personality transformation begins with our thoughts.

- When we interact with people, let us interact with the soul, the pure being, rather than the acquired body, positions and achievements. When we talk through the consciousness of our acquired labels, then it is the ego of one talking to the ego of the other.

- In any situation, we are playing our role along with so many actors. Let us stop writing their script because they are not in our control. Instead let us write only our script. When we keep thinking of what others are doing, we are only depleting our own energy.

Creating My Destiny

SO: Sister Shivani, we were speaking about thoughts and awareness. I realize that by the time I am aware of something, the action has already taken place. Thoughts come and go so fast that it is slightly difficult to be aware or be in control of them; yes, one thing has happened that when I am getting angry, I can stop in the middle of things. I am waiting for the awareness to happen before the anger triggers.

SS: You know this is a very good start, to be at least aware. You are able to stop there in the middle, which means if earlier you were going to stay out of control for 10 minutes, now you will be able to probably finish in a minute or so.

SO: Something within me reminds me, talks to me, to take control of myself.

SS: Because we have changed our definition of what is natural. Earlier we said anger was natural; so we gave ourselves the liberty to get angry. Anger was needed to get work done. That was our belief system. Our anger was justified so we did not find the need to change. Now we are experimenting with a new belief system. Peace is natural and we want peace; and now we understand that it is our own sanskar. Now when you get angry, you understand that you are doing something that is not your natural self, and you realize and stop.

SO: We left at a question in the last chapter. What would people say – look, he is a weak man, the other person said so and so to him in public but he kept quiet.
SS: First, let's see what is more important: how I feel or what people feel. This is a very big question. We need to check carefully, it will be different for each of us. For some their own personal well-being is more important and for some, other people's opinion matters more.

SO: I will say both, but honestly mine is more important.
SS: Let's visualise a scene, two colleagues in an office. One of them is screaming and hurling abuses at the other one. The opposite person reacts in the same manner and shouts even louder. Would we call this strength? Now in the same situation, the second person remains calm and stable, understanding that it is not the right time to explain his perspective. Not only does he remain composed outwardly, but even empathizes with his colleague and retains his good wishes for him. If you are a spectator to this scene, would you call this weakness? Let's not even think whether it is strength or weakness, let's just see which behaviour is more sensible and easier. If someone shouts at us, is it easier to shout back or to remain

internally stable and retain my right thoughts and feelings for the opposite person who has just shouted at me?

SO: The second option is very, very difficult.
SS: So that's where strength comes in.

SO: And you think doing something difficult is strength.
SS: Yes, because it requires strength to do something difficult. I have to pick up this whole chair, it requires strength. I say I can't do it; it's my physical weakness. To do something against the tide, of negative energy, to remain protected first and then create positive energy against the tide of negative energy requires a tremendous amount of strength. To shout back and say he shouted at me first, what kind of strength does that require?

SO: In school we used to get bullied. If we kept quiet, we would be called a sissy. You are not a man, people would say.
SS: When we are bullied, we are quiet but internally we are disturbed. If the boss shouts at me, I can't say anything back because of his position. But internally I am not stable; it starts having an impact on me. People will say that I may as well shout back and finish it off; it's better to get angry rather than keep my anger inside. Here we are not talking about keeping our anger inside; we are simply not creating that turbulent energy; that is strength.

SO: Sister Shivani, it's so difficult these days to say a word to your boss. Everyone wants to retain their position. People hear so much from bosses, but internally they are in pain.

SS: So they are already creating anger. It's a silent anger, it's internal. Anger is anger, whether it is in the form of hurt, in the form of hatred, or in the form of verbal abuse. It's having an effect on you. But once I start taking care of my thoughts and feelings, I will be able to stop outside first and gradually will stop creating it inside. Then it will not matter whether it's my boss or my child; the rule remains the same.

SO: So, to experience unlimited happiness what should one do? How does one acquire this kind of mental stability?
SS: First, understand that anger is not strength; it's absolute weakness because in those moments I have gone out of control, and going out of control is not strength.

SO: If anger is not strength, what is anger? Is it a void? Is it frustration or an inferiority complex?
SS: Anger is the whole turbulence that takes place inside; I justify it and I blame the world for what I am feeling, and I want to get back at them. The anger could be because of one person and it might come out on another one. We give vent to our anger in various ways and towards various people. You say I can't say anything to the boss; so when I come home I shout at my wife. My wife can't say anything to me, so she goes and shouts at the child. So I can't say that I didn't get angry at all; it's just that I accumulated it inside at the moment when things were heated. I didn't vent it but then I created it, and eventually took it out on someone or the other. Let's understand this mechanism. Probably then, I will be paying a little more attention to what I am doing in my life. Every time I create a thought, what's the next thing that happens?

SO: After the thought will be the action.
SS: That's a later stage. What happens just after I create the thought?

SO: When I create a thought, I am creating certain emotions within me.
SS: Yes. Immediately after I create a thought, the next thing that happens is the feeling. Sometimes we are not aware of our thoughts but we are aware of our feelings. I am not feeling very nice today; I am not sure which is the thought that I created but I am aware that I am not feeling nice today. Or I am feeling very nice today; whatever I am feeling, it's because of some thoughts that I created. So, if I am not aware of my thoughts, let me just be aware of how I am feeling today because the feeling is only a result of the thought. I have to meet you…this is a thought that I will create. Based on my past experiences or what I have heard about you, it will immediately generate a feeling. Thought is always followed by a feeling.

All my feelings put together about you, about the world, help me develop my attitude. A thought about you is followed by a feeling subsequently; and because this has happened many times, an attitude towards you is also created. You know, when we talk about 'changing our attitude', it is about changing the thought. How can I change my attitude? I have to first change the thoughts that I created.

We cannot change our attitude. We have to change the thoughts, and our attitude will automatically change.

SO: And to change the thought?

SS: That's what we have been talking about—sit back, check, choose and change.

SO: Awareness and practice. And awareness itself is practice. Being aware, being aware, being aware all the time, that's the practice.
SS: And gradually you will find that your attitude has changed.

SO: You won't have to think of anything because then it is automatic.
SS: It is in the process plant.

SO: So the base is the awareness of your thoughts.
SS: There is a stage before that which we will see, but let's consider the subsequent stages first... thought, feeling, attitude, and action. If I have a positive attitude towards you, my way of talking, my way of behaving and what I do with you will be different; but if I have a negative attitude, everything will be different.

SO: When you said action, do you know what you remind me of ? My director calling out 'action' and I starting to do my scene! He says 'cut' and I stop.
SS: This is something we can do throughout the day – action and then cut. In your profession at least you have a retake, but in normal life we don't have a retake. The action is already done. When shooting, despite the retake option you pay so much attention. In life, where there is no retake, we hardly pay attention. Every thought that I create has an impact on me and my body and the people around me. For 10 minutes

112

I have created thoughts of pain, and in the 11th minute I say 'okay, enough now, let me change but those ten minutes'. That's why there is this need for constant awareness. It happens with practice. The 10 minutes will become 8 and 5 and 3, and then finally it will be 'okay, this is it'. And then we will reach a stage where we will not be creating it; we will be aware of it as soon as we are about to create it and we will say 'okay, change'.

SO: And one day it won't get created at all.
SS: Yes, because then I have come into the consciousness of my original self—that of a pure being. We are now in the transition stage. It's like we are sleeping and trying to wake up. We wake up a first and say 'okay, let me sleep for five more minutes'. We wake up to the truth and say I am a peaceful being; and then we create anger once more, that is we fall asleep again.

SO: One has to believe first. If I tell somebody tomorrow that you are a peaceful being, he will ask me what the proof is. Is it because everyone yearns for peace?
SS: You only yearn for that which you are. The body is made of five elements of nature: water, air, ether, fire and earth. Whenever there is lack of one element in the body, we immediately say 'I want water', 'I want fresh air'. Why do I want fresh air? Why do I want water? Because the body is made of this and it's lacking these right now. At that time if you give me anything else, I will say no. Similarly, I the being am made up of seven elements: purity, peace, power, love, knowledge, truth and bliss. Every time there is a little

imbalance, we say: I want peace, I want happiness, I want love, I want power.

The method may be different but everyone is looking for the same things because those are what each one of us is made of. I can be using anger as a tool but I am never comfortable when I am angry. Anger is not my nature; anger is an acquired 'sanskar', an acquired personality trait.

SO: Probably that is why we like a peaceful person, a peaceful being. We like to sit with a saint, and feel at peace in a particular temple or shrine, or under a tree.
SS: Because we have come closer to our natural self. We go to a scenic place to see the sunrise or the sunset, to feel nice. Stuck in the middle of a traffic jam, we don't feel nice. Why? Chaos is not our natural self. A place or person or a situation that makes us feel closer to what we actually are, makes us feel nice as well.

SO: So all these seven elements are me and this is the proof that whenever I am at peace I am happy. How does one get the battery recharged for all these seven elements?
SS: Try to understand the process completely. Now I am changing my thought from 'I want peace' to 'I am peace'. Thought changes, feeling will change, attitude will change, and action will change. Now my actions will not be focussed on seeking peace, because now I know that I am peace. My actions will be coming from my discovered nature of peace.

Any action repeated a number of times becomes a habit. All my habits put together make up my overall personality. So who I am today, the personality is a package of every thought we create. Personality development programmes teach us to talk like this, smile like this, say hello like this and so on, but they will not work if we are not happy inside. How can I keep smiling if I am not happy? And even if I am smiling, what energy am I sending out? So, personality begins in the mind. So it is thought – feeling – attitude – action – habit – personality. Now, we come to the last and most important step. This personality goes out into the world, working, socializing and being with family; at every step I am creating my destiny. And it started from my thoughts.

SO: Oh! So thought is creating destiny? And life is a manifestation of one's thoughts? I am creating my future, I am creating my life, and I am creating my environment. I am getting back what I am giving. Today it all starts from a thought and it envelops our life, our future, our destiny.
SS: And then we would do anything to change our destiny today. We can go to an astrologer, to a numerologist, to a tarot card reader. We want them to predict our destiny, and if it's not what we like, then we ask them to do something to change our destiny. The truth, though, is no one can do anything.

SO: How can we change our thinking?
SS: First step is to understand how important it is. Earlier we would say that they did this to me so I have to get back at them. But now we take care that what we think and do will create our destiny. We are so confused today about destiny; we say this happened to me; it's my fate, my luck. But fate decided by who? Since we don't know who it is, we just

115

point the blame somewhere up there and say God decided this for me, again putting the responsibility on someone else because we are not ready to take the responsibility. The fact is I am creating my destiny. The energy that I send out is my 'karma' and the same energy when it comes back in the form of situations or people is destiny. When we go to an astrologer and he tells us to wear a particular ring because things will be much better then, we obey and wear the ring. When we wear the ring we create a thought naturally that now things will be better for us, and things are actually fine because we use the ring as a stimulus to change our thoughts, and thereby change our destiny.

SO: So it comes to having faith in that ring.
SS: Yes. If I wear the ring without faith, it will not work.

SO: A holy person tells us that he will write this particular prayer, put it in a 'taweez' and you wear it around your neck, then no black magic or any evil is going to afflict you. We are so sure that nothing will happen to us now. So our thought has changed.
SS: For how long are you able to create that thought after wearing it? If we are not aware, this thought will be there for a few days; after that the ring or taweez is just a part of the body.

SO: I never thought of this point. Now somebody gave me this ring and I am wearing it; for a few days I am aware. I think if I wear this, all my negativities will be gone and I will be a happy person. I forget it after sometime and go

to my actual nature. I haven't changed myself at the core.

SS: You used the ring as a stimulant to change your thought. Until you are aware of the ring, you are creating the right thought and the belief that 'now everything will be okay, no one can do anything wrong to me'. This was the thought that was required, with or without the ring. But because you are wearing the ring, faith in the ring makes it easier to create these thoughts. One month down the line it's a part of your body and again you will go back to your same old thought process—'they did this to me, they did that to me.' When you forget that you are wearing the ring, then the effect will not be there.

SO: So stimulus is creating the thought.

SS: Stimulus is not creating the thought; I am using the stimulus to create the thought.

SO: I am creating my own thought because of the stimulus. So you want us to do the same thing without this ring?

SS: You are doing it, the ring is not.

SO: Do you have any meditation on this, that I am the power and I am creating it?

Relax and Reflect on these thoughts. Meditate.

My life ... my journey... I am writing the script ... as I create every thought ... I am writing my own destiny ... let me be aware that no situation is happening on its own... I have written my destiny... Whatever is happening to me now ... I had written the script for it much earlier... What I am doing now ... what I think now... I am writing my script for my present and for my

future... The control ... the power is totally with me... Let me be awake and aware that I am the scriptwriter of my destiny... I the powerful being... I am not influenced by situations and people ... focus and attention on my thoughts manifesting into my destiny. Om Shanti!

MANTRAS FOR HAPPINESS UNLIMITED

- If other people are behaving in a reactive manner, at that time for me to remain stable internally, is strength, and hence Peace is strength not weakness.

- Anger is not strength. It is a sign that I have lost control on myself. Even hurt, resentment, are silent forms of anger, and damage me the creator.

- My every THOUGHT is followed by a FEELING. So if I am not feeling nice, I have to stop and check – what have I been thinking.

- My feelings over a period of time, created on the basis on my thoughts, develop my ATTITUDE – about people, situations, work or about the world.

- My attitude comes out into ACTION. Any action done repeatedly becomes my HABIT. All my habits put together is my PERSONALITY. At every step in life this PERSONALITY determines my DESTINY.

- I the being am an embodiment of 7 qualities – Purity, Peace, Love, Bliss, Knowledge, Power and Truth.

The Energy of Consciousness

SO: Sister Shivani, you have said life is a manifestation of one's thoughts. You also mentioned astrologers and people who predict your life or give you a ring or an amulet to wear.

SS: We need to understand it in the right perspective. Everything that is guiding us in how to lead our lives or is predicting our future—whether it's astrology, numerology, or some other branch—is a science. People have studied that science over a period of time and have acquired a sound understanding for it. It's like a doctor who has studied the body. Let's say I consult a doctor with my blood tests and he says there is a probability that in the future I am at risk of getting diabetes. It's an assessment based on my genetic factors, my current lifestyle and on the present condition of my health. I go back home with the new information. There are two ways of responding. One, 'I am going to have diabetes; it's going to happen because my mother has it, my grandmother has it; I have so much stress and my lifestyle is very erratic. The doctor also says that I am going to have diabetes.' So if the doctor said that I can get it in a year most likely if don't take the right measures, then with such a negative attitude it is possible that I will get it within six months. The stress that I create with the doctor's information will precipitate the disease. Ultimately, I will say that what the doctor said has turned out to be right.

The other option I have after I receive this information is to take complete charge of myself. I bring about a shift in my lifestyle, I start meditating, I start 'pranayam' and yoga. I change my food habits and sleep timings. I start walking. I take care of my emotions and then continue leading a holistic lifestyle. There is a great chance that I will never have diabetes, and the assessment will not come true.

It's a response to an assessment acting like a prediction. The probability was there, so that was pure science. There was a probability of my getting diabetes, but it was still a probability; not a reality. I picked up that probability as a warning signal and brought about a shift in my lifestyle. The assessment was then not true because I took charge. But if I don't take charge and I just accept the probability as a reality, then it is going to become the reality. I have accepted it already, I have created anxiety and worry, and so it is going to happen because the probability was already there.

In the same way, I go to an astrologer. He says based on the planets, the moon, the stars, the positions right now, there is a probability that this and this and this will happen in the next six months or the next two years. There is a probability of your physical health getting affected, of your business facing some obstacles, of someone trying to harm you. It's only a probability; it's not a reality yet. This is very important to understand, that it's a probability predicted by someone who understands the science. So we thank them for making this prediction and giving us the probability, but now we take charge.

SO: So you mean to say we should take it as a warning and then like we did for diabetes, modify our lifestyle, and see to it that the prediction or the probability doesn't come true.
SS: Yes, but only if we have the power to listen to the information and not get influenced by it. What happens unfortunately is that when somebody gives us the prediction, we accept it as reality. We say this is going to happen because the expert has said this, and the expert's predictions for so many people have come true. It's going to come true in my case as well. We have already converted the probability into a reality. Our mind accepts it that this is going to happen. Thoughts create destiny and so it happens.

SO: Earlier the expert's predictions might have come true many times. So that may be a reason for us to believe in him.
SS: True, because it's pure science and there is nothing wrong about the prediction. It's a probability for the one for whom that prediction was made; that person accepted the prediction as reality. His mind accepted it, so it manifested as reality.

SO: But don't you think that knowing the prediction will

change the destiny?

SS: There are two ways. Let's say someone predicts for me that my next six months are going to be very challenging; the planetary movements are not favourable. Whatever I do, I am not going to be successful. It's a prediction. If I don't know this prediction, I don't know this piece of information. So I put in all my efforts, obstacles come but I overcome them, because I am all motivated to work. I want success and I am working for success. Obstacles come but I don't get demotivated. The other option is I know the prediction that success is difficult to achieve in the next six months because planet movements are not favourable for me. The information is so powerful for me that I am not able to raise my thoughts beyond it. I start my business but I say 'what's the use, I know it's not going to be successful in these six months. Whatever I do there is going to be a problem.' Even when I am faced with the smallest obstacles, I say that this was going to happen, and I lose my enthusiasm needed to overcome the obstacle.

SO: So, it is safer not to have this piece of information.

SS: Either you don't take the prediction, or if you know the prediction then raise your thoughts beyond it, and go above that prediction. Take it as a challenge.

SO: I am peace; I am bliss; I am knowledge; I am powerful.

SS: Absolutely. Now where is the obstacle? The obstacle can be only something outside. The only thing that is required to face an obstacle is stability inside.

SO: Even a child falls so many times before he learns how to walk.

SS: The important thing is that when he falls he gets up and starts walking again. Now let's suppose somebody has predicted that you are not going to get up for the next six months, try walking how much you want, you are only going to fall. The first time you fall, you say 'forget it, I will try after six months because so-and-so has told me that these six months I cannot walk'. So you don't even try with the right energy, and because you don't create the right thoughts, you don't get the right destiny.

On hearing the prediction we ask them for a solution, so that we can be successful in these six months. Then we are told wear this particular colour, wear this particular stone. What happens? Do the planets change? No, they are still there. But we are doing something that is helping us to change our thoughts. First we had the information that these six months would not go right for us, and so we were demotivated. Now we have the information that if we wear this particular stone, success is certain. We create the thought that I am wearing the stone and now let any obstacle come, I am going to cross it. I will get through the phase while I wear this stone.

SO: People talk about the rays of the Sun passing through the stone and going inside the skin. What about that?

SS: I, the being, is energy. I have vibrations. As will be the qualities of the being, love, peace, purity, so will be the aura of the person. The photographs of deities always feature a white light around the head; it's a symbol of the purity of the soul. So if the soul is pure, the aura is white. If there is some conflict somewhere, the aura is not going to be white or cream or yellow—it could be red, blue, or grey. By using an outside stimulus, we try to change the colour of the aura, which then will have an effect on the mind. So we are going from outside to inside. The easiest way will be to change my thought; automatically the aura will change, vibrations will change, situation will change.

SO: Basically the colours and stones are changing our aura?
SS: Yes, these too work, but how much, to what extent and for how much time? Someone tells you to wear a red colour shirt and things will be better; how often can one wear a red colour shirt? Why not just create powerful thoughts instead? We always thought that the easiest method was to change something outside so as to experience a change inside; it's actually about changing something inside to experience results outside. The process is inside out, not outside in. The inside is in my control and is a permanent change.

SO: When you do it from outside, you do not have complete control. People who predict something are not entirely right. It happens often that you will call them and say that you said this to me but it didn't happen', he will probably say, 'Sir, I am also a human being and cannot always be correct.'
SS: They were not predicting reality; they were predicting a probability. We have to remember this. We have no right to say anything to them. A probability will always have a percentage. They may even predict that your next six months

will be very nice, but if you are demotivated inside, nothing is going to be smooth. So the prediction is going to be wrong.

We have been discussing about the effect of external influences on our mind. We are practicing to enable our mind to go beyond the influence of situations, objects and people. If my mind can go beyond the influence of situations and people, then we can also go beyond the influence of planets. Planets are also an external influence. They do have an influence, but it is up to us whether to get overpowered by it, or to rise above the influence. When we are weak internally, everything will have an influence; someone's smallest word will disturb me because I am weak. The mind doesn't have the power to cope with, accommodate and pack up all the thoughts, so your one word can upset me for the next one day or for the next six months. If your one word can upset me for the next six months, the planets' movement can also upset me for the next six months. It is all about rising above external influences.

SO: Basically it is on me, whether I should be disturbed or not.

SS: Yes. You know it's like this room is in so-and-so direction, so the husband and wife will never get along well in this room; change your bedroom, change the particular wrong direction into the right direction as directed by the expert. But is it necessary that everyone whose house is in the right direction has a good relationship? No. If this had to work, then everyone would just change the direction of their house, wear the stones, and all would be bliss. Many of us are doing all of that, then why is there so much pain and failure?

SO: But it has worked for people.

SS: For some time. They create the thought 'I have done this, now my relationship will work'. Six months down the line, they would have forgotten that they changed the direction of their house. North, south, east, west, these are energies, magnetic fields. It is a field and it will have its effect, but the highest field is here (in the mind). If we say that we can get along with each other come what may—north, east, south, west—and then we actually can get along. We can then get along even in the wrong direction of the house. And if we cannot get along, then we cannot do so even in the best designed house. It's about the mind ready to take the challenge. We cannot always keep changing everything outside; okay, I can change the house, but can I change you? I can only change the way I think.

SO: But they will give you good examples of how this direction has got energy.

SS: Because it's science; there is no doubt about that. But there is a science, an energy that is much higher than the energy of alphabets, numbers and planets. It is my own energy, the energy of consciousness.

SO: Am I not weak here, when I use some other energy? I have a much stronger energy within me?

SS: I can't take charge of my mind, so I take charge of everything else outside. What time I should begin my business; in which direction should my office be; which stone should I wear; which symbol should be put in my office. I can just take care of everything around me because I don't have the power to take care of my thoughts.

SO: I have the bigger power here within and I am going with a begging bowl to smaller powers.
SS: The weaker we become, the more we will go outside. The lesser control I have on myself, the more my power is reducing, because I am not taking care. If you don't discipline your child at the right time, he will get spoilt eventually.

SO: What is the care one should take?
SS: Discipline the mind, be aware, take care, and choose the right thought.

SO: Somewhere it is very important to understand who I am, how powerful I am. If I am peace, I don't say 'want' anymore.
SS: Yes, I don't have to do anything to be peaceful.

SO: Then I don't say 'please give me some power'. I am power, I am knowledge. If I am so much, and there is such abundance, why will I need anything?
SS: We will not, at least not anything external. Everything external is needed for physical comfort; it's needed for fun, for excitement, for entertainment, but not for peace and happiness.

SO: So if I am going for a holiday. What should be my thoughts? Earlier I used to get disappointed that I took my family for a holiday to make them happy, but my child came back unhappy.

SS: Be happy and then go for the holiday. Not go for the holiday to be happy.

Because I am not going on the holiday for happiness; I am going just for fun, for a change from the daily routine. That's all that a holiday is. So the holiday will not be for pursuing happiness; it will be for expressing and sharing the happiness that we are filled with. The perspective changes from taking to giving, so then we look forward to meeting people, we look forward to being with everybody, so that we can radiate our happiness to them, not so that they can make us happy.

I am a peaceful and happy being, but I get to experience it and express it only when I am in interaction with someone. If I am sitting by myself, I don't get to express or experience my own qualities, and that's why relationships are so important. Unless I am in interaction, unless I have this exchange of energy, I will not be expressing and experiencing. I experience my quality only when it comes out. When I give anger to you, first I experience it; similarly, when I give peace to you, first I experience it. I get to experience it only when I am in interaction with someone and so I look forward to going to work; I look forward to meeting families and friends– not for wanting but for expressing and experiencing, and therefore sharing.

SO: How much lighter one must be feeling when he is not doing it artificially and things are just happening! See this difference between doing and happening.

SS: We are "human beings" but today we have become "human doings". We are doing so many things. We are human beings, so let us be what we are supposed to be first. Spirituality says 'be happy and do this, because you are a human being doing action'.

SO: Human being doing action... Let's bring the whole thing into a small meditation.
SS: Relax and Reflect on these thoughts.

This body is my costume ... it is just a machine... I am the controller and the operator of this machine... Consciousness ... energy ... the spiritual being ... my original sanskar is purity, peace and happiness... Let me look at myself ... consciousness at the centre of the forehead ... the operator sitting there taking charge of this machine ... playing roles ... relationships and responsibilities... I the human being doing action ... but as I do... I express what I am... Let me look at myself driving to work ... at office with my colleagues ... at home with my friends and family ... with the awareness... I am a pure being doing things ... interacting with people ... and thereby expressing and experiencing my original sanskar of peace and happiness... Let me see how the day will be. Om Shanti!

MANTRAS FOR HAPPINESS UNLIMITED

- People predicting our future are only telling us a probability. It is only a probability, not a reality.

- We have the power to listen to the prediction and still choose our response – that is, our thoughts and actions – and thereby create a reality based on our choice.

- We always think that we need to do things outside to change the way we feel inside. The reality is we need to change how we feel inside to change the things outside.

- Happiness is not something that we should expect to get from other people – it is to be created within and shared with people we meet.

- We are not "human doings" doing things to be at peace; we are "human beings" at peace and doing things.

Everything Happens Here
(In the Mind)

SO: Sister Shivani I was reading, "What comes first: peace or happiness? Can you be at peace if you are not happy? Do you get happiness from external factors or from within? The mind is fickle like a fast galloping horse and the only way to control it is by involving it in good actions beneficial for all." I need your help to understand this.

SS: The quotation says – "When you are at peace, you will be happy depending on what your idea of happiness is, whether you get it from outside or from inside". Let us stop and check what outer happiness is. It's not outer happiness – it's an outer stimulus which I use to create happiness for myself.

SO: I like the way you say, 'I create happiness'; emphasis is always on our creation, you never say, 'it gives me happiness'.

SS: At every step, when you are happy, when you are hurt, or when you are upset, just stop and ask who is creating it. I am creating it, irrespective of whatever the situation or the stimulus. The more we are aware we will understand that we have lived all our life saying you are responsible, whereas all the time it was we who were creating it. So that is the awakening. Now we only need to take care of how can I change what I am creating?

Without this understanding, we would feel powerless because we believe people are responsible for our happiness and people are responsible for hurting us. We would wait for people to talk nicely to us. At the same time, hope that they will always be nice to us. What if tomorrow they don't talk nicely to us? Then we will not be happy. There is dependency, and hence fear. When we understand that everything is happening here in the mind, then there is no insecurity and there is no fear of the future. So situations could be pleasant or not so pleasant, and people could be pleasant or not so pleasant, I only have to take care of one person and that person is me. It's very simple.

The other thing that you mentioned was about the mind being fickle and the only way to control it is by engaging in good acts that are beneficial for all. Fickle means when the mind is indecisive and inconsistent. When the mind keeps changing, the quality of thoughts is not very nice; when we are peaceful, the mind works slowly and cautiously. When we are worried, the thoughts are very fast; when we are stable, the speed is slow; when we are fearful, the thoughts gain speed. So if my mind is fast and inconsistent, it means the quality of energy is not right. And now we want this mind to do an act that is for the good of others. Benevolence is not in the act, it is first in the energy that I send out while doing the act. Here again, by asking you to do a benevolent act that will control the mind, which is running haywire, we are putting the stress on 'doing something outside which will help you to be peaceful'.

SO: But either way it works, doesn't it? Suppose I am in a bad mood and I start dancing; it changes my mood. Your mind is at least not as agitated as before, so you can take a better decision. What I mean to say is even the outside-in approach works to a certain extent?

SS: Outside-in works to an extent and for some time. Like people say when angry count to ten. When we are angry, we don't even realize before we react. If we had that awareness that now I am angry, I need to stop and drink water and count numbers, we would be aware enough not to react.

SO: So we come back to just being aware.

SS: Yes. These are only little-little things given to us so that we can pause, take a break, and work on our mind. Like you said, if I dance for some time at least my mind will be in a better position to understand. So you have just given your mind a little gap; I am upset with something but instead of confronting you right now, I take a little gap. Now what is that little gap for? So that I don't confront you right now. I postpone my external reaction. The internal reaction is there; I resolve the issue internally and then I decide how to respond. There is a difference between the reaction and the response. Reaction: automated and not in my control; response: think, understand and then respond. That's why we try and bring in those time gaps, but sometimes, in fact quite often, the reaction is so fast that the time gap is lost.

SO: I remember when I was in business there were so many letters I used to write in anger in the night, after I had closed down my office. I used to keep the letters for the next morning to post, but I never used to do it.
SS: The mind is moving at a very fast speed, so postpone your reaction till the speed slows down. See the situation in a different perspective and then you may respond in a different way. This is what we were trying to do right now. And what we are trying to do now is keep the mind at a slow speed always.

SO: Again you go back to awareness.
SS: Yes. If you are aware, the speed is slow. Imagine that you have a child playing in the room. If you are not looking at the child; the child will do whatever he wants. He is dropping things and breaking things. Now just stand in the corner and watch the child. Don't say or do anything, just watch the child. He will become aware and will control his activities.

SO: I try to watch this child (or mind) inside so much but he finds some place and escapes.
SS: That's the journey, and it's not going to happen in one day. Have you been able to do it sometimes?

SO: Yes.
SS: That's the proof that we can do it.

SO: Somewhere my mind doesn't like this kind of an exercise.

SS: A child never likes to be disciplined because he is used to running around wherever he wants, doing whatever he wants. Suddenly I say I am going to take charge of you now; now you are going to do only what I want you to do. But then, gradually the mind will get used to this way of thinking because it's going to be at ease. Even the mind is tired now; it's been running at a very fast speed.

SO: Can we switch it off like we switch off the engine of a car?

SS: We are not able to switch it off even when we are fast asleep at night; forget switching off in the day time. We need to understand why the mind works like this. There are certain influences on the mind. We know about positive thinking, yet negative and waste thinking comes naturally. What are the factors that influence the quality of thoughts? In any situation, at any time, whatever thought I create is influenced by three factors. One factor is past experiences. If I had an interaction with you before, if I had done business with you before, I have a past experience. Every time I think of you, my quality of thoughts will be based on those past experiences. If it had been a pleasant experience then nice thoughts come to me. Second factor is information – everything that I take in through my sense organs. What I read, what I watch, even what I eat, everything that is going in has an effect on the mind; information plays a vital role on the mind. Now, the first thing in the morning the mind is very clean; it had a good rest of six hours; it is fresh and ready to

135

create, and ready to absorb. In the morning we usually read the newspaper first or switch on the news channels. We are reading, listening and watching about terror, violence, natural calamities, financial issues, social and political upheaval, etc. The mind which is like a clean blotting paper absorbs this troubling information. The kind of information will influence the thoughts. Information is the food, thoughts are the resultant energy. If I have eaten the right food, I am going to be healthy; if I have not been eating the right food for the mind, my emotional immunity system is going to suffer.

SO: So that means whatever we are taking in, through media, through the surroundings, the quality of our thoughts is dependent on them.
SS: Negative information will give rise to negative thoughts; that's definite because that's the raw food that I have taken in. The thoughts are creating the destiny that's the mechanism inside, but what's creating the thoughts is the raw food, which is information. So, if I want to take charge of my thoughts, if I want to change the quality of my thoughts, I will have to first change the quality of the raw material that goes in. During the first two hours of the morning the absorption power of the mind is very high. If we are reading, watching and listening to only negative things during this time, and then we want positive thinking, from where and how is it going to happen? Then, tonight if our child hasn't come back home on time and his phone is out of range or switched off, it's so natural to think that something must have happened to him or her. We need to assess why we feel that something could have happened to him or her. Why are we creating a

thought that is negative?

SO: What kind of energy are you sending into the universe?
SS: Yes, we have to wait for half-an-hour and we still can't get in touch with the child. What is going to be the quality of thoughts as we wait or in any other situation like that? Then we will say – *'Is it not natural to think negative. How can we just sit back and say everything will be okay?'*

SO: Can't we think of another way that he must have met a friend and made other plans or he must have gone for a movie and the network is low there?

SS: How often are we able to think that someone is late because something nice must have happened? That's a question mark. Negative thinking comes easily because that's the information we have taken in. Even if we start with this simple practice of not watching the news or reading newspapers early in the morning, it can bring about a big change. Protect yourself; do not feed yourself with so much toxic food in the morning. Just this simple practice will bring results.

SO: Then you cannot blame situations because you yourself will be responsible.
SS: Situation is a trigger; the information is filled inside. When this trigger comes, the quality of the thoughts created will be influenced by the quality of the information.

SO: First we take in wrong information or negative information, then we start thinking negatively. And when

the child comes home, we pounce on him. Why are you late? What happened? I was so worried.

SS: Why do you pounce? You pounce because in that one hour that you waited you were creating negative thoughts. This stimulant has just come and we think he is responsible for all that we created, so there it goes. How much toxic energy have we created in that one hour of wait? We sent vibrations to the other person and spread it to everyone around us in that one hour, and then we say isn't it natural. No, this is not natural. Natural is he has not reached; I am not being able to contact him, and the situation is not in my control. Let us always see immediately what is in my control and what is not. If the situation is in my control, take charge; but if the situation is out of my control then there is only one thing in my control, it is the quality of my thinking.

SO: But tell me one thing: why is it easier to create a negative thought rather than a positive one?

SS: You just have to fill in a different quality of information. It's as simple as that. When I change the quality of the information coming in, the thoughts change, the way I respond changes, and my destiny changes. I have a choice. When the newspaper comes in the morning, I have a choice as to what time I will read it. So let's just postpone it; let's take this one resolve today. There will be a big change. Postpone the newspaper and the television news to the later part of the day and substitute it with something very pure and powerful. A simple change to your morning diet for the mind will make all the difference. So one positive thing in the morning, and one positive thing just before going to sleep is the remedy. What do we take in just before going to sleep? Television serials? A horror movie? That's the last layer of information going with us. It will affect the quality of our thoughts during the night. The first layer of information in the morning influences our thoughts during the day. The last information before we go to sleep influences the quality of our thoughts at night.

Let's devote 10 minutes to reading something pure and powerful after we have finished our duties for the day. We have to fill in the information first because if we just sit and try to create positive thoughts we won't be able to do it.

We have to change the last layer of information. Once we finish reading, we will sit back and reflect on that, unpack what has happened for the day. That's very important; let's not sleep with unresolved issues. Go through the day. Situations had come up and there were times when we did not respond in the right way. Reflecting on the day does not mean reflecting on all that happened. Instead reflect on the way we responded and see how we could have responded in a different manner.

SO: So sister, will you teach some meditation right now for the evening, before we go to bed?
SS: Relax and Reflect on these thoughts.

Let's sit back, with the body relaxed... Just before going to sleep ... let me look at the day... An entire movie has passed scene after scene ... with lots of actors around me acting according to their scripts... Let me not get entangled in the situation... Let me just watch myself playing the role ... as a detached observer... I will just focus on my performance ... let me not look at the other

actors in the scene ... no judgement or comment... I am looking at myself ... my response and my script in every scene... As a detached observer let me ask myself ... was there any scene that I could have performed differently... Did I have another choice to the way I was writing my script... Let me play the scene again on the screen of my mind ... same scene but a different me ... with a different script... I am programming my mind and preparing my mind to a more powerful and a positive response for the next day... Om Shanti!

MANTRAS FOR HAPPINESS UNLIMITED

- People say when angry, count one to ten; these are external measures to postpone our reactions. However, if we take care of our thoughts we will not create even the thought of anger.

- Our thoughts are created based on our past experiences and the information that we take in through our sense organs.

- During the first few hours in the morning, the power of the mind to absorb information is very high. We need to take care of the quality of information we take in then. To protect ourselves from creating negative thoughts, we need to avoid newspapers or news channels or anything that has some disturbing information to offer early in the morning.

- Let me try a new way of living, to be able to create pure, powerful, positive thoughts naturally. Let me begin the day by reading or listening to pure and positive information.

- The last layer of information at night influences the quality of my thoughts while sleeping. So let's finish the day with a few minutes of reading or listening to pure and pleasant information.

The Colour of My Thoughts

SO: Om Shanti! Sister Shivani, how important is a belief system for happiness?
SS: We have seen the whole process that takes place inside – where every thought that I create gives rise to a feeling and the feeling develops my attitude. The attitude comes out as action; repeated action becomes habit; habit develops my personality; and my personality determines my destiny. This is the process from thought to destiny. The point is that every thought becomes very important. But what determines the quality of my thought? Everyone is talking about positive thinking, so why does the negative come so naturally the minute there is a stimulus or a trigger? The factors that determine the quality of our thoughts are past experiences, information in which we saw the impact of media, television, newspaper early in the morning and late at night just before going to sleep. These two play a very important role in the quality of our thoughts. The

third and the most important factor is our belief system. Our body is like a computer, I the soul is the operator, and the belief system is our operating system. As will be the operating system, so will be the way the software will run on the machine. We generally say this software will run on this particular operating system, while that one will not run on another operating system. This machine is important, the operator is important, but the operating system plays a very important role. At times there could be a virus in the operating system, which is also a certain belief system that may hamper the way I think and thereby my destiny. Spirituality will help me to install an anti-virus. Many people use a computer but do not install anti-virus in the machine, so time and again the system tends to get corrupt.

SO: They also don't see its expiry date.
SS: Yes, you need to update your operating system. What is the sign that my system crashes once in a while? Outbursts of anger, pain, or being hurt are signs of a system crash. It's time to understand and check how often is my system crashing in the whole day.

SO: But there are so many people who are irritable throughout the day.
SS:: And then they will say this is natural, this is my natural behaviour, this is how I am.

SO: But they also insist that somebody else has passed the virus on to them.
SS: Even if someone passes the virus in me, it's still my

responsibility to have the anti-virus. No one else is going to come and put the anti-virus. Times are getting tougher, situations are getting challenging, people are becoming increasingly unpredictable. Suppose I have known you for years and suddenly there is a change in your temperament and your behaviour changes. I have known you to behave in a particular way and then suddenly I say I don't expect you to behave like this. Let's say your nature is jovial and carefree, but suddenly you are confronted with an issue. You are going through some conflict in your life and your temperament changes. I am used to you talking to me very openly and light heartedly. Now I can't understand why you have withdrawn. You are not communicating properly.

SO: So what is your duty and my duty then?
SS: My duty first will be to take care of myself and not get hurt. You see, that is where friendships and relationships suffer. If I get hurt first, then I am sitting and nursing my own wounds. If I am hurt because you did not talk to me properly, I cannot help you. I take it personally, and start feeling you are angry with me and you do not respect me anymore. While I am creating all this pain, I do not understand that it is not about me, but your behaviour is because you are in pain for some other reason. Since I am in pain, I will not be able to help you to heal

SO: But why is the other person's behaviour so important for us?
SS: Public acceptance, appreciation and approval from people around us. The magnitude will vary, but acceptance and

approval from people around us seems to be the foundation of our self-esteem.

SO: Sister Shivani why is it easier to misunderstand than understand?

SS: We misunderstand because we are hurt. We are in pain, and when in pain we will never see the situation in the right perspective.

SO: What you say is right but it's easier to misunderstand than understand.

SS: Your shirt is white in colour. But if I wear different colour glasses, it will appear a different colour to me every time. You are who you are, but if there is a different colour, or perspective every time because of my pain, my hurt, my ego, you will appear different to me. So it's a misunderstanding.

Clean your own windows. Don't ask them to change their shirt.

SO: That's what you meant by morning meditation and before-sleep meditation. That is also part of cleansing.

SS: Absolutely. Any blockage, any negative thought, and I will look at everyone through that window. If I have been hurt because of something that happened with you and I am in pain, I carry that pain with me to everyone, and I will see everyone through that pain. If I have been rejected by you and my self-esteem is low, my self-esteem will be low with everyone. It's not that my self-esteem is low when I am with you and high when I am with someone else.

145

SO: I think some people do make you feel comfortable. They also raise your self-esteem.

SS: But we cannot be dependent on people to lower or raise our self-esteem. If I find five people who can help me to raise my self-esteem, I may find fifty who can bring it down.

SO: That is why people find their own comfort zone and own groups and own people and own friends.

SS: But who is the comfort zone? Even within family and friends there are many who will lower our self-esteem.

SO: So even within twenty family members we select only four or five. I am comfortable here, but I am not comfortable there because they lower my self-esteem. Our topic itself is 'happiness unlimited', and here we are limiting ourselves.

SS: Again, let's say being with you raises my self-esteem because you accept me unconditionally. But you are able to do that only when you are in a stable state of mind. Tomorrow if you go through some problem, you lose your capacity to accept me unconditionally.

SO: Not only if I am in a problem. Suppose today I accept you as you are, but tomorrow I do not like what you do, then my behaviour towards you will change.

SS: Absolutely. I was feeling very nice with you until today, but now I have to prove myself to you. And as soon as I start to prove myself, there will be fear. Are you happy with me? Have I been able to prove myself right? And because I am in this constant process of proving, I am in fear and so

I am not sending the right energy.

SO: In the final analysis we come back to the point that one has to be independent.
SS: "In-dependent": dependent only on that one who is inside; let's not be "out-dependent" because outside things will change and they have a reason for changing.

SO: Does that make you a little recluse?
SS: Remember always that to heal and to help others, I will have to be healed first. If I am healed, I will always be there for other people; if I am not healed and I am in pain, I can never be there for other people. I have to first take care of myself to be there for others selflessly.

SO: So this is selfishness in a positive manner.
SS: This is the foundation for being selfless. Today even when we are doing something for others, it is less with the intention of giving and more with the intention of taking. Even while doing for others we are satisfying some vacuum within ourselves, so it is actually being selfish.

SO: So caring for the self is necessary so that we can take care of the others.
SS: The equation flows this way – only a healthy person will be able to heal others, will be able to understand others. Without understanding my own thinking, my attitude, I want to understand why you are feeling like this. How is it possible? I am not ready to understand why I am hurt, but I want to understand why you are upset. And the wonderful

part is when we understand how our mechanism works, understanding others becomes easy. If I am hurt I will immediately be able to realize that I am hurt; I understand the reason and check my attitude, now it's up to me how much time I want to remain like that. If I am jealous, I will immediately come to know that I am jealous. Now if I see someone who is upset, I can go beyond the visible hurt to see what must be happening inside for them to behave like this. It becomes easier to be with people; you don't look only at the criticism, you look at the dynamics inside this person's mind for them to be so critical. So we just have to understand our mechanism – then we can understand everyone else's.

SO: This remind me of an incident that happened in the society where I live. One of the neighbours was angry, shouting at everybody and ready to fight. I told one of my friends, also a neighbour, that this person's behaviour was obnoxious and that I could not stand it. You know, this is what she said: 'what about him, poor chap, look at what he must be undergoing! He must be in some kind of pain to behave like that.' Now I understand what she meant. Understanding others is very difficult. If my wife's behaviour changes, I never ask her if something is wrong. I just get irritated and leave her alone to manage it herself. Why couldn't I ask her if she needed any help?

SS: This is withdrawal. When we can't handle other people's temperaments, we withdraw. Even if it is temporary, even if it is for one hour, when the other person is in pain we withdraw.

Think of your wife getting angry or behaving in a slightly different manner; it could be a sign that she needs help. At that time you move one step behind. You think when she is fine you will come back, but that's the time when she needs you more. It's because you are not able to take care of yourself that you move away. This is not support; we are not there for each other emotionally, though physically we are living in the same house. We are not there to heal each other because we have not healed ourselves.

Suppose you are sitting with a friend and your son walks into the room; he has come from outside, doesn't wish you or your friend who is sitting there, and he just walks past both of you. What's the first thought that comes to the mind? What's wrong with him? Where are his manners? What is my friend going to think? He will think I haven't brought up my son in the right way. Will the friend go out and tell others how my son is? What will everyone else think about me? So we are nursing our own wounds. My responsibility is to not to question why the child is behaving like this, but see what is the pain inside that caused him to behave like that. Now you will go to his room and question his behaviour. Your child will request you to leave his room and leave him alone. When the parent has been hurt or felt disrespected, the child will not want to be with the parent. Right now the child is in pain, and he doesn't want to be with anyone else who is in pain.

You will love to meet somebody who is absolutely stable and is accepting you unconditionally, extending unconditional support. We don't get this from too many people, in fact from hardly anybody. Unconditional acceptance means I do not fluctuate irrespective of your temperament and I am not judgmental about you. Then the energy that will flow from anyone who accepts us unconditionally also helps us to heal our wound.

SO: We fluctuate automatically. If you raise your voice, I raise my voice; if you are soft, I am soft; if you smile, I also smile. Such complicated lives we live.
SS: We keep changing our behaviour according to everyone else. Because of this, we tend to forget our original qualities. My sari is white in colour but if I meet somebody in red, I paint it red, when I meet somebody in black I paint it black, and when I meet somebody in green I paint it green. At the end of the day there is no white left. So where is my personality? I coloured my personality according to everyone else's personality. And it's actually not their personality either; it's my perspective about their personality. We don't know people as they actually are.

SO: Actually we are not capable of knowing.
SS: Because we are seeing them through our perspective. There is only one person who knows me well and that's my own self. No one can claim to say that they know me very well – no, they know me through their perspective and that perspective keeps changing.

SO: So a child knows his father from his perspective.
SS: Absolutely. The same father will get along with his three children in different ways because the children see the same father in a different perspective. One might be very scared but

that's because he or she is weak; one could be very confident and could run and get onto his lap; one will just stand in the corner neither scared nor very confident. The father is the same, though his nature and personality is the same. So if one is comfortable, why are the others scared? One is a meek personality, so he sees the same father through his perspective.

SO: Sister Shivani, let's consider a normal couple. If a husband is tough, the wife says 'can't you be nice some time', 'can't you speak softly', 'can't you be loving', and so on. Conversely, if a person is very loving and soft, his wife will say 'can't you be tough sometimes, look at what that fellow said to me'. Even from your perspective, you are not happy with one kind of role your partner plays; you want them to play different roles all the time.

SS: Because we have created an image of who the right husband is. We get into a relationship with the image of an ideal partner and an ideal friend, and then we spend our life time trying to change our partner into that image. Let's say my image is that of a partner who is an extrovert, dynamic and loud. But I have a partner who is very soft and quiet, and an introvert. According to me, this is not how my partner should be. So it's not about how he is as an individual; it's about what image I created in my mind. I will keep on saying this is not how you should be, you should be loud, you should be more open, you should be like this, you should be like that. Then if he becomes an extrovert, I will say, not that much, a little less. So I want the person to be exactly the way I want him to be. It's like going to a tailor and the tailor prepares your costume according to the measurement that he prefers. He tells you that now you have to change your body and fit into it. He expects you to fit into the costume that he has made rather than creating the costume according to your measurement.

And that's why we keep fluctuating. We keep changing according to what everybody wants.

SO: We fluctuate because of them or because we are not stable?
SS: What will happen if I meet ten people and I feel my happiness is dependent on making these ten people happy? They will all expect me to be a different kind of person. If I keep changing, where is my original self? Inside I will get suffocated because I am struggling to change.

SO: To come out of this struggle, not be suffocated, and be stable, can we have some kind of a meditation?
SS: Actually in every system there is a core that never gets corrupt. That's the consciousness. Meditation is the process of passing those layers of belief system and reaching that core which is the spiritual energy.

Relax and Reflect on these thoughts. Meditate.
*Different people I meet the entire day have different personalities...
each one is operating through their belief systems... their rights...
their wrongs... their perspectives...*
  Let me look at myself ... through which perspective do I

interact with each individual I meet... Is it an influence of their personality... am I changing according to everyone I meet... or am I able to hold on to my internal, pure, original personality... Let me look at myself today the entire day... meeting about twenty people... Let me see myself with each one of them... interacting through the core of my personality... my original sanskar of purity and cleanliness... I the flawless, perfect, pure being...uninfluenced and undisturbed ... by anything and anyone around me. Om Shanti!

MANTRAS FOR HAPPINESS UNLIMITED

- There is only one person who knows me well and that's my own self.

- Be "in-dependent": dependent only on that one who is inside; because outside things will change and they have a reason for changing.

- Our thoughts are created based on past experiences, the information we take in and most important our belief systems.

- Its important to take charge of how we feel, instead of being dependent on others. To be INDEPENDENT means to be dependent only on the one inside.

- Let us be ourselves and not keep changing our behaviour according to the way others behave with us.

To Heal You,
I Have to Be Healed First

SO: Sister Shivani, what about our past experiences influencing our mind.

SS: We cannot avoid our past experiences. They are already recorded in the memory, but we can try not to play the same record again and again. Because every time we play it, we are converting the past into the present. We are creating the same emotions all over again, and every time we create the same emotion, we deepen the 'sanskar'. We deepen the wound, by scratching it. It's a past wound, we need to heal it, but suppose we open the Band-Aid from time to time and scratch it, how will the wound get healed. Sometimes we also get others to join us. So the wound never heals. The past has passed. Full stop. No comma, no question mark, no exclamation mark. Why, what, how... Full stop. So that we are able to move ahead, fresh and clean, and now what we create, will get recorded. People say we remember the past because we have to learn from the past, but what do we have to learn from the past? We just have to check the way we responded and learn if there was a more comfortable way of responding. There is nothing to learn from the situation, we only have to learn from our response. Holding on to things, not letting them go, accumulating, it is only going to cause pain. It's like you are holding on to something; the weight of the object remains the same but the longer we hold it, the more the hand is going to hurt.

SO: Hurt! People get constant headaches, skin diseases, and no doctor knows what's happening.
SS: Because they are holding on to it. Remember, it's over. It's the past, not in my control.

SO: What should one do? Suppose something very sad has happened in my past and it comes to my mind. A friend comes and asks what the matter is, and I share with him about what took place in the past.
SS: That's what is meant by opening everyone's Band-Aid together and scrubbing on the wounds. We went through so much of pain but when we think about it again, we experience the same pain all over again. So we need to ask our self: how many times am I going to go through the same emotions again and again? More importantly anything done repeatedly becomes my personality, and then I carry that personality with me everywhere. We may not discuss the past situation with everyone, but because it's in our mind it will be part of our vibrations.

155

SO: But don't you also attract such people and such situations?

SS: We are not attracting situations, but we are responding to situations in a similar manner as before. If there is a challenge, since we are already emotionally low, we don't have the power to face the situation in a proactive way. I am already hurt about something that happened years back, and here comes another fresh stimulus. I don't have the strength. The pain that I will create will be much more than what I would have created had I healed my past. Also pain created because of one particular situation or person, does not remain only in that relationship with that person. The pain has now become a part of my personality, and I will tend to get hurt more easily in other relationships too.

SO: So it is link after link after link.

SS: Because it's my personality, not theirs. I can use you as the stimulus and say I am hurt, but now it's my personality. This personality will go with me to every situation and every person. So I am vulnerable every time. It's not about changing your job, it's not about changing your partner, your friends, your spouse; it's about making yourself stronger.

And then your immunity system, your emotional immunity system, is strong wherever you are, with whoever you are. It doesn't matter who and how they are.

SO: Do you think it's easy for people to change their thoughts?

SS: People are doing miracles with their lives. They are doing it; no one else is doing it. The first realization is – IT'S ME,

NOT THEM. We are responsible for how we feel, no one to blame. I have seen couples who were on the verge of divorce coming back to a happy married life with only one understanding – it's not him or her, it's me I have to work on. Things change.

SO: In a divorce it's a blame game.
SS: In a divorce it is usually about 'you are wrong'. Now we understand, it's my response to the situation, irrespective of his or her behaviour, and then we start focusing on our response.

SO: They will say 'if you speak like this, then naturally I will respond like this'. How do you still change?
SS: So that is the realization. 'You speak like this', but now I will choose how I am going to respond. The equation has changed. I got a phone call from a twenty-four-year-old married woman, standing on the terrace of her house wanting to jump down. As a last resort she just called up and said, 'I don't want to live and I was about to jump down, but I thought I will just call up and find out if you have a solution. My husband is having an affair with somebody in the office and he wants to divorce me. I see no reason to live'. She was totally shattered. 'What about my parents, society and others?' At that moment I was speechless. I said, 'Okay, first come down. So what is it that you want?' She said, 'I want everything to be back to normal like it was. I want my family life, my married life to be what it was'. I said, 'create a thought that everything is fine'. She said, 'but everything is not fine'. I said, 'I know, but what do you want?'

'I want everything to be fine'. I said, 'now create a thought that everything is fine and my husband is absolutely fine; nothing wrong has happened'. For 10 days or so, we were talking daily for almost an hour on the phone. She used to say, 'everything is not fine, how can I create this thought that everything is fine? What should I do? Should I go and talk to that girl? Should I go and talk to that girl's parents? Should I go and talk to my husband's parents, what should I do?' I had to repeatedly get her back to creating the same thought, that everything was fine. Finally she started working on changing her thought; she said 'everything is fine, my husband is absolutely fine, nothing wrong has happened'. She stopped crying also, eventually she became more stable. Now when her husband came back from work, she wouldn't be crying or weeping; this provoked him even more. He would be abusive and find more faults with her because he was trying to justify his own action. She had to remain stable and just keep telling herself that 'everything is okay, I am in charge of the situation, and I am in charge of myself'. After one month her husband handed over the divorce paper to her; he said that his company was sending him to the USA and that the other girl working in the office was also going. They were going to get married there. She called me up and told me what happened. Then she surprised me by saying, 'you know I am fine, I think I will be able to take care of myself. I will take up a job and I will be able to live with my parents'. In one month she had changed her thoughts. The situation was the same as it was one month before, but she had changed her thoughts. She just worked hard on herself. The husband left.

Two months later he called up from the USA and said he wanted to come back. She called me up and asked 'what should I do?' I asked, 'what do you want?' She said, 'I want everything to be back to normal'.

SO: That's what she always wanted.
SS: Yes. And today it's more than four years since that episode. They have a lovely daughter too. All the effort was made by her. The knowledge that we learn at Brahma Kumaris and the simplicity with which it can be implemented, can be adopted by everyone. It's only that they have to take up the challenge; it's a little extra effort initially.

SO: Did you feel a sense of failure when the husband was leaving the next day and they did not patch up?
SS: It was not a failure. We were not looking at the situation; we were only concerned about her being able to take charge of her own state of mind. Situations are not in our control. We expect that spirituality or religion will change our problems. No, they won't. Problems are going to come, challenges are going to come, obstacles are going to come; spirituality gives me the power to take charge of myself and then face the situation.

SO: But when she was creating the thoughts that everything is fine, she was trying to change the situation
SS: She was changing her thoughts.

SO: By changing the situation in her imagination.

SS: It's not imagining. Everything is fine here (in my mind); it's here first. I have to be okay; everything is fine.

SO: But what kind of visualization did you give her? You said 'just think that everything is fine; nothing is wrong'.

SS: If a partner or a child is drifting away in a relationship, what's the energy that we send out to them? Anger or hurt. Someone is already drifting away and we are sending out negative energy. It will only take them further away. If you want the person to come back, you have to send powerful positive energy. For that we need to stop being critical and judgmental about that person. We need to respect them as we always did, and so we need to create the thought that nothing wrong has happened. From the other person's perspective, they have logic for what they are doing; we may find it wrong but they have a reason. I have spoken to so many families where there is a conflict between partners or between parent and children. If you talk to both parties, you will never be able to decide who is right and who is wrong because none of them is wrong. You listen to one and you will say, 'perfect, this person is absolutely right'. Then you listen to the other person and what they say seems to be making sense as well. It's just that each one is right from their own perspective. Now all that we have to do is show them each other's perspective.

SO: We can approach the situation with understanding and knowledge.

SS: I will tell you about this couple. The wife had been living separately for the last three months because the husband used to beat her. The physical violence had been happening for 10 years; finally she took her daughter and left. She met me to see if any solution was possible. She was constantly weeping while she was talking about it. I asked her how her husband's childhood had been. She said it was not pleasant; he was a single child to working parents, who did not have much time for him, and he had been very lonely. What I understood was that the husband felt he had not got love from others around him; in his wife he found one person whom he could call his own, and the way he showed power and control over his wife was violence. It was actually because he was insecure and possessive, and he was in a lot of pain inside. Now, instead of hatred she was filled with sympathy. She said, 'my husband was in pain all this while, and I thought I was the one who was in pain'. This reality changed her, and now they are healing each other. It's not that the situation is solved in one day because the husband says he doesn't know what happens to him. Such things happen because of some mind block inside. It's just that we need to be able to detach ourselves from our position, go to their position, and see what could be the reason for their behaviour. But what happens is when the husband does something wrong to the wife, the wife goes into her own hurt. She fails to understand what the husband is going through, and vice versa.

SO: What if both of them had a bad childhood?
SS: The wife was constantly weeping. She kept telling the husband 'promise me that you will never hit me again, only

161

then will I go home'. The husband said 'I promise I will try'. She said 'no, give me a guarantee that you will never do it again'. So I told the lady, 'you guarantee that you are never going to cry again'. She promptly said 'I will try'. It's so easy to tell other people to change because we don't have control over our own 'sanskar'.

SO: But can we change the 'sanskars'?
SS: Yes, definitely, by understanding and seeing what the reason is.

SO: How can I find the reason within me? It takes "you" to find it or can "I" find it? Suppose I get angry very easily; how do I know what kind of 'sanskars' I have? Will I have to go through my past?
SS: Definitely you need to see your past. Suppose someone has had a troubled childhood – the parents were critical, physically abusive, etc. The child always has to keep proving himself, and still keep going through pain because of the criticism received. Now as this child grows up, he builds a defense mechanism. He does not want to go through the hurt and pain, and so he becomes loud and aggressive. Before anyone can say anything to him, he will shout at people. People will fear him. This is a protection wall that the person builds so that no one can ever say anything to him, but inside he is an innocent, fearful and hurt child.

SO: He had gone through some situations that he could not fight.
SS: Not only that, the child experienced hurt at that time.

Now the child doesn't want to get hurt again, and this will be so even when he is 30, 40 or 50 years old. Now when this person starts working on himself and says I will not get hurt even if someone says something, he becomes strong inside. Now he can drop this artificial defense mechanism and be his natural, polite, sweet self to everyone.

SO: So all these things can be overcome by being aware of your thoughts. By being aware, you also detach, don't you?

SS: Absolutely, because we get detached our self from our own perspective. Like in the case of this couple, the wife could see only her perspective, 'how can my husband hit me, he does not love me, he does not respect me'. What she is feeling is right, but she can see only her perspective. When she detached from her perspective, she was able to see her husband's pain and his perspective; she became stable. Her hatred turned into sympathy.

We all talk about understanding people. We say we cannot understand the other person, which means we just cannot see their perspective because we are so attached to ours.

Earlier we could see the situation only from our side, and from our side it was totally different. For me to be able to see from your side I have to get up from this chair and then come and sit on that chair. For that I have to detach myself from this chair; I am so stuck to my position, to my ideas of right that I can't even get up from here. When I get up to be on your side, that's empathy and understanding, and that's a relationship.

SO: You were mentioning the other day that when a person is empty within, he becomes angry. What do you mean by emptiness within?

SS: Vacuum. Many people will tell you that they have everything in life, professionally, personally, materialistically. But inside there is something amiss. They are not even very sure what they are talking about.

SO: You mean to say there is some kind of a search, some kind of an emotional fulfilment they are looking for?

SS: All that we were doing, studying, working, achieving, even our relationships, we were doing it all to get happiness and contentment. At the age of 30 or 40, we realise that we have got everything but we are still experiencing stress, anger and anxiety. So I am empty in the sense that what I wanted I haven't got, even though I got the whole list that I thought would give me contentment. Then I say I am empty. While achieving this success, we compromised a lot. That compromise made us empty. Peace is our nature, but we created anger. Honesty is our nature but we compromised on that a number of times in order to achieve success. Humility is our nature but created ego to feel powerful. Every time we were doing these things, we were going against our natural personality.

SO: So you feel bad about it, perhaps guilty too.

SS: Not only feel bad now, we think of how the journey has been. Let's say this glass is full. Now I am on a journey towards success but I have to take care that the glass should not spill. If I keep spilling the glass during the journey, some

10 years later I would have achieved success but the glass will be empty by the time I reach there. Then I will say that I am empty because I created so much anger and resentment. I did everything possible to achieve that success. It doesn't mean that success is wrong; just that I should have taken care of this glass while moving towards success.

SO: But even before moving towards success we were empty, weren't we?
SS: No, look at a child – so contented. That's what's so attractive about the child. We teach the child that in order to be happy he has to get more marks; in order to come first he has to get tensed and compete with his friends. Look at the child when the child is sleeping – such serenity.

SO: Can we meditate to sleep like a child?
SS: Relax and Reflect on these thoughts. Meditate.

Let us sit back and relax ... preparing myself for a good sleep... Let me just look at the day ... everything that's passed is past ... full stop... However tough ... however challengin g... it's over... Now is a new moment ... a new response ... and a new feeling... I am in control... I am pure energy... I am already complete ... beautiful ... contented ... successful... Everything that I was looking for outside is already there in me... The purpose of my life is not to achieve it outside ... but to express it while I am moving through my goals... I the complete ... perfect ... pure being ... master of the body and every sense organ ... everything in control. Om Shanti!

MANTRAS FOR HAPPINESS UNLIMITED

- Every time we think of the past, we are making it the present because we are creating the same emotions again.

- The past is passed. Full stop. Let it not repeat in the mind; when you do, it is like rubbing a wound and therefore not allowing it to heal.

- There is nothing to learn from the situation that happened. The only thing I need to learn is whether I had the choice of responding in another manner.

- Holding on to the past – not letting go – will only create pain within. The situation is the same but the longer we hold on to it, the pain increases.

- In relationships, no one is ever wrong; each one is right from their own perspective. Detaching from my own perspective and understanding the other's perspective is empathy.

- While working towards our achievements, if we take care not to compromise on our values of peace, love and happiness, we will be always contented.

Brahma Kumaris

The Brahma Kumaris is an international NGO in general consultative status with the Economic and Social Council of the United Nations and in consultative status with UNICEF. With its global headquarters in Mt. Abu, Rajasthan, through more than 8,500 centers in over 120 countries, the Brahma Kumaris offer a wide range of courses and programs to create positive change.

The Brahma Kumaris teaches Rajyoga as a way of experiencing peace of mind and a positive approach to life. The organisation provides opportunities to people from all religious and cultural backgrounds to explore their own spirituality and learn skills of reflection and meditation derived from Rajyoga, which will help develop inner calm, clear thinking and personal well-being. In the past seven decades the organisation has made values like purity, peace, love and joy a practical and sustainable experience in the lives of millions of people worldwide.

At the heart of the organisation's teachings is the foundation course in Raja Yoga Meditation. This course provides a logical and practical understanding of the relationship between spirit and matter, as well as an understanding of the interplay between souls, God and the material world. All courses, seminar and workshops are offered to the public free of charge, as a community service. www.bkwsu.org (International), www.brahmakumaris.com (India)

PEACE OF MIND channel is a 24 hours TV channel of the Brahma Kumaris.

COURSES OFFERED

- Self Management

- Stress Free Living

- Living Values

- Emotional Intelligence

- Mind Management

- Harmony in Relationships

- Self Empowerment

- Developing Concentration Power

- Increasing Memory Power

- Enhancing Self Esteem

- Exploring Inner Powers

- Values in Health Care

Self-Realisation – Recognising the self as a spiritual being, an infinitesimally tiny star, point of light – a soul. The intrinsic nature of the soul is that of love, peace, happiness, truth, bliss, purity.

Knowing God – Like us, God is also a soul, the Supreme Soul – who never takes a body of His own. He is the Almighty Authority, the Ocean of Love, Peace, Power and Purity.

Relationship with God – When you learn to tune your mind in meditation to the mind of God, then whatever the situation, you always have a source of help and strength to draw upon – an infinite reservoir of power and virtues that is only a thought away.

Law of Karma – Whatever circumstances I am in at the moment – is the consequence of my own prior thoughts, decisions and actions. But if the past created the present, the present also creates the future.

The Foundation Course in Rajyoga Meditation is offered at every centre of the Brahma Kumaris. It is a 7 day course, 1 hour daily, free of charge. To know your nearest centre visit www.bkwsu.org (International), www.brahmakumaris. com (India)

BRAHMA KUMARIS CENTRES

The Brahma Kumaris have more than 8,500 centres in over 133 countries, with the International Headquarters at Mt. Abu, Rajasthan.

INDIA

World Headquarters 'Pandav Bhawan',
Post Box No.2, Mt. Abu – 307501
Tel: 2974 – 238261 To 238268

Om Shanti Retreat Centre,
Gurgaon. Tel: 0124–2379960

Shanti Sarovar Retreat Centre,
Hyderabad. Tel: 040–23005983

25, New Rohtak Road, Karol Bagh, New Delhi.
Tel: 011–23628976

23, Dar-Ul-Muluk, Gamdevi, Mumbai.
Tel: 022–23803681

81/1, Bangur Avenue, V.I.P. Road Side, Kolkata.
Tel: 033–25747863

3702, Annanagar, Block Q–96, Chennai.
Tel: 044–26267441

UNITED KINGDOM & EUROPE

Global Co-operation House, 65–69 Pound Lane
London. Tel: 44–20–8727 3350

Global Retreat Centre
Oxford. Tel: 44–1865–343 551

Centre de Raja Yoga, 74 rue Orfila Paris, France.
Tel: 33–1–43 58 44 27

Raja Yoga Institut
Frankfurt, Germany. Tel: 49–69–49 18 46

Styrmansgatan 3 Stockholm, Sweden.
Tel: 46–8–663–79 59

12 rue J.-A. Gautier Geneva, Switzerland.
Tel: 41–22–731 12 35

RUSSIA

2 Gospitalnaya Ploschad
Moscow. Tel: 7–499–263 02 47

4 Severny Prospect
Saint-Petersburg. Tel: 7–812–293 28 44

NORTH & SOUTH AMERICA

Global Harmony House, 46 S. Middle Neck Road
New York. Tel: 1-516-773 0971

Peace Village – Learning & Retreat Centre
New York. Tel:1-518-589 5000
2428 Griffith Park Boulevard
Los Angeles. Tel: 1-323-664 0022

1212 New York Avenue
Washington DC. Tel: 202-238 3263

897 College Street Toronto, Canada.
Tel: 1-416-537 3034

Rua Dona Germaine Burchard, 589
Sau Paulo, Brazil. Tel: 55-11-3864 2639

AFRICA

Global Museum, Maua Close Nairobi, Kenya.
Tel: 254-20-3743572

Inner Space, 28 Judith Street Johannesburg, South Africa.
Tel: 27-11-487 2800

ASIA

17 Dragon Road, Causeway Bay
Hong Kong SAR. Tel: 852-2806 3008

1-30-15 Numabukuro Tokyo, Japan.
Tel: 81-3-5380 4169

52 Lorong Melayu Singapore.
Tel: 65-6441 1411

Harmony House, 10, Lorong Maarof Kuala Lumpur, Malaysia.
Tel: 60-3-2282 2310

Chaengwattana Rd. 27, Pakkret
Bangkok, Thailand. Tel: 66-2-573 8242

7484 Bagtikan Corner, Makati City
Manila, Philippines. Tel: 63-2-890 7960

AUSTRALIA & NEW ZEALAND

78 Alt Street, Ashfield
Sydney, NSW. Tel: 61-2-9716 7066

4 Park Avenue, Avalon
Wellington. Tel: 64-4-567 0699

Brahma Kumaris

24-Hour TV Channel

Peace of Mind For Peaceful Life...

On:
- **TataSky:** Channel no. 192
- **Airtel Digital:** Channel no.686
- **Videocon d2h:** Channel no. 497
- **Reliance Digital TV:** Channel no. 171